T0090471

Becoming a
HEAVENLY
WOMAN

THE ULTIMATE BEAUTY MAKEOVER

CAROLYN MACMAHON

WESTBOW
PRESS®
A DIVISION OF THOMAS NELSON
& ZONDERVAN

WestBow Press books may be ordered through booksellers or by contacting:

WestBow Press
A Division of Thomas Nelson & Zondervan
1663 Liberty Drive
Bloomington, IN 47403
www.westbowpress.com
844-714-3454

ISBN: 979-8-3850-0327-3 (sc)
ISBN: 979-8-3850-0328-0 (e)

Library of Congress Control Number: 2023913336

Print information available on the last page.

WestBow Press rev. date: 08/23/2023

DEDICATION

This book is dedicated to my husband, Thomas, who lovingly walked with me throughout my spiritual journey, and to my mother, who lived a life of grace and beauty before me.

I also am indebted to all the women who became friends, as we took the paths together through the Bible toward becoming Heavenly Women. Some of these have been so encouraging to me. Here are some of their responses to my cover art, depicting a woman traveling heavenward as she finds her beauty in the words of the Bible:

The path of the righteous is like the morning sun, shining ever till the full light of day. Proverbs 4:18—Judith Cantrell, Hot Springs, Arkansas

You make known to me the path of life; you will fill me with joy in your presence, with eternal pleasures at your right hand. Psalm 16:11—Tammy Yoakum, Cottonwood, Arizona

Your word is a lamp for my feet, a light for my path. Psalm. 119:105—Joanne Johnson, Mena, Arkansas

I see, the Word is a light for my path—Naomi Patton, Cottonwood, Arizona

It reminds me to walk in the light, and with grace—Natalie Cooper, Searcy, Arkansas

That person is like a tree planted by streams of water, which yields its fruit in season and whose leaf does not wither— whatever they do prospers, Psalm 1:3—Mary Lee Goss, Phoenix, Arizona

I absolutely love this piece. A wonderful inspiration. My heart has been touched by the Bible art. Each time I see it I get a special feeling that I can't really put into words—Barbara Adams, Dallas, Texas

Carolyn, this is your best art! You can't achieve beyond this—Lisa Whitley, Dallas, Texas

I truly love this one. The very best is ahead of us! We're marching upward to Zion, the beautiful city of God!—Barbie Hatfield Goudy, Mena, Arkansas

Narrow is the way that leads to Life, Matthew 7:14—Tonya McDonald, Mena, Arkansas

Every book is a journey. Open the pages and see into the heart and mind of the author, take a journey through their thoughts and memories. To me, you have brought this thought to life, given it a visual definition. As far as a biblical perception, opening your mind to the perusal of others in their journey, is a gift and a calling from God. As is your art. Lovely! He leadeth beside the still waters, He restoreth my soul—Maggie Payton, Mena, Arkansas

Light arises in the darkness for the upright, Psalm 112:4, Be still and know that I am God—Faith Lewis, Custer S. Dakota

I really love this!—Mary Hatfield Pontius, Mena, Arkansas

BEGINNING

I started out the way most girls do: I was 17 and I thought I was in love. It must have been love, because it was so exciting. The captain of the football team courted me with flowers and letters and gifts, and during Freddy's freshman year at college he surprised me with an engagement ring. We planned a storybook wedding at a dreamy little ivy-covered stone church with a steeple and a bell, in a darling little town. I made my own gown of "candlelight satin." I loved the sound of those words! We—perhaps I should admit that it was I—planned the perfect wedding, the perfect honeymoon, and then happiness ever after, probably in a flower-covered cottage with a picket fence.

I was so unrealistic! I knew absolutely nothing about making a home in such a cottage, or what it means to join two single lives into one to form a family. All I could see was the wedding, the happily ever after. I didn't have a clue even about how to do laundry! As an older woman now looking back, I imagine that the laundry was probably the farthest thing from his mind too! Guys usually envision a sweet wife to hug, while women dream of long talks and meaningful thoughts; I'm betting that neither is focusing on laundry.

If only we had spent as much time talking about our expectations of each other and of marriage as we did the color of the silks and the flavor of the wedding cake! Or even if we had spent as much time actually worshiping in the church we were to be married in. How I wish I had been interested then in seeking God about this very serious move, and about His plan for a marriage. But, like many girls, the fairy tale was all I could think about. I was chosen by Prince Charming!

My first big disappointment in my fairy tale was my fairy godmother. It started when my fiance announced one day that he had bought our first home. Surprise—a house trailer! He had picked it out with his *mother*! (I saw red at that, for some reason.) They had it put in a trailer park near his mom, for us to move into after the wedding. He thought I would be thrilled. I was stunned. *What, no flower-covered cottage? No picket fence?* I tried to look excited, but it was no use. I couldn't explain—or didn't—and all he could tell was that I was disappointed. Wasn't the fairy godmother supposed to take me to a castle or something, or at least a cottage? But the godmother turned out to be his mother and a *trailer?* Oh, now I'm old enough to know that what Freddy and his mother had done made sense for a boy with three years of college left: get a place we could afford and get on with school. He didn't know about the romantic scenario girls have in mind, as most men don't. They really are at a loss as to how to please us, and often we are at a loss to explain it, so the relationship breaks down early on. At least ours did.

We hadn't even gotten married yet, and I was sulking. *His mother picking out my house?* Somehow it seemed her fault that we would have to live in a trailer. I never even thought in those days about where the money came from for the down payment on the trailer! Later on I suspected that it came from that same mother! I was an immature, silly girl, totally unrealistic, totally unreasonable; but to me it was all very real, real enough to shake up my world. Freddy and I didn't fight about it, but seeds were planted then that grew to be weeds. (Funny how things roll around: many years later, I made the down payment on our son's house, and our daughter's too! I picked it out, I remodeled it. It never occurred to me that the daughter-in-law or son-in-law might consider my generosity "interference.")

Mothers-in-law can be hard work at the best of times; mine got off on the wrong foot to begin with, although with the best of intentions. One thing I have learned that keeps peace in a marriage is to each insist that the other spouse frequently call or visit his or her own mother regularly, and never speak unkindly about the spouse's mother. Even if a man were to complain about something his mother did, down deep he really doesn't want his wife to agree. Same with me: I knew well my parents' faults, but I didn't want to hear it from my husband. However, that was long ago, and I didn't know the mother-in-law rules yet.

The second big shock came as life settled down after the wedding. The flowers, gifts, dates, and dinners out mostly stopped. Here is where I made a huge mistake, and I think most brides do too. We don't know the difference between courtship and marriage. There *is a* difference, and rightly so. I've heard it said that in the "hunter" man's eyes, after the chase of the hunt is over, we gals are "the bagged game." That sounds so crass. Let's try to be more generous about it: he has successfully completed the courtship and won the fair maiden's hand. OK, men are practical, and once they complete a project they go on to the next one. Freddy's next goal was schooling, so he redirected his focus and poured himself into his studies, no doubt a very prudent and smart thing to do. However, all I could see was that his world no longer revolved around courting me.

I remember one time, early in that poorly-planned marriage, that I was missing the attention I used to get on dates. I fixed my hair just so, made my makeup perfect, put on perfume and a new outfit, then paraded by his chair where he was studying. He didn't look up. So I went by again. Still nothing. After going back and forth a few times, he finally looked up but just asked, "What?" I felt cheated. And mad. But I wouldn't tell him why; instead, the classic line we women use came out: "If you don't know what's wrong, that's even worse!" Then, after some stony silence, probably a day or so, we had a big fight over it. No wonder King Arthur sang "Who can understand a woman?" when trouble was brewing in Camelot.

Looking back to those days, I try to imagine what he must have thought. Here he is, preparing for a college test, and life is peaceful in the trailer-house. Then his bride, the one he had thought was so sweet and wonderful, comes into the room. She seems to be coming back and forth—perhaps she has lost something. He looks up and inquires, but she clams up and gives him the silent treatment. Then she dissolves into tears about how disappointed she is in him. He does what most men do at this point in the marriage: he retreats. Men usually avoid talking about feelings and relationships, so when things get tough they go into their emotional "cave" and become increasingly unreachable. The woman tries harder to cry and shame and bully him out of his cave, but it only gets worse. He feels that he not only doesn't understand what she wants, but he is pretty sure he will lose in a war of words and ideas.

My dream world was shattered. I know now that because it was an unrealistic world, *it had to be shattered*. I also know now that most brides go though this to some degree or another, and need help understanding what is going on. You may be a new bride, or a woman disillusioned with marriage but resigned to it, and are wondering if anything can be done. There is hope and help, but you must understand this important thing: *we all need to get a make-over!* We are all born naturally selfish and rebellious, which is harmful for all relationships, but especially toxic in a marriage. The good news is that God has a *real* beauty makeover in mind, tailored just for you! He knows how to make you into an ideal woman—a *heavenly woman!* It isn't hard; if you listen to God's advice, He will get you there. The journey may take you in directions you never dreamed, but you will become a heavenly woman. I promise!

I will share my story, bit by bit, chapter by chapter, each dealing with one aspect of our heavenly makeover. There will be some of God's advice (scripture), some of my mistakes and lessons learned, as well as a LIVING IT section to help you access your own makeover. Finally, each chapter will have a FOR FUN bit: extra down-to-earth things that we all can enjoy along the way.

What woman doesn't love a makeover? This one will be the best ever. Let's get started.

Chapter 1

THE NEW WOMAN:
AN AMAZING BEAUTY
MAKEOVER

I was a painfully shy child, skinny, with thin brown hair like a scarecrow on a bad hair day. My sister, just two years younger, was one of those blue-eyed, pink-cheeked little girls with golden curls and dimples, and I preferred to fade into the background when she was around. Actually, I didn't have to hide; I felt invisible next to her. If someone had told me then that I would eventually become a professional color consultant doing beauty makeovers for large groups and on TV, I would have thought they were mistaking me for my sister.

However, God's ways differ from our ways, and here I am, very cheekily telling ladies how to be beautiful—God surely must love to laugh. Here was the girl nicknamed Squeaky because of her mouse-like voice, all grown up, giving beauty makeovers, and advising the best colors and styles for each person.

Some people might consider these to be vain things, but I never did. How nice it is to hear how the old-time prophet Ezekiel spoke of a beautiful bride:

> I also clothed you with colorfully woven cloth and put sandals of fine leather on your feet; and I wrapped you with fine linen and covered you with silk. I adorned you with jewelry, put bracelets on your wrists, and a necklace around your neck. I also put a ring in your nose, earrings in your ears, and a beautiful crown on your head. (Ezekiel 16:10–12 NASB)

These Bible verses tell you that God Himself likes His bride to have beautiful clothing and jewelry. He had a unique plan for each one of you, even down to choosing what your coloring would be:

> For You formed my innermost parts; You knit me [together] in my mother's womb.
> I will give thanks and praise to You, for I am fearfully and wonderfully made;
> Wonderful are Your works, and my soul knows it very well.
> My frame was not hidden from You, When I was being formed in secret,
> and intricately and skillfully formed [as if embroidered with many colors] in the secret place. (Psalm 119:13–15 ESVA)

Beauty makeovers are always fun. Women are attracted to the idea of a "new look," somehow thinking that if they could have a *real* expert help them, they would be transformed. The Bible has a lot to say to us about this!

Actually, God Himself has a real beauty makeover in mind for each of us, and He is the expert who promises to do it! We are unique—God's masterpieces—but we somehow miss being what He designed us to be. In a *spiritual* sense, we all need to be transformed to become our best selves. In the *natural* realm, many of us also end up wearing the wrong colors of clothing and makeup. We are not naturally heavenly women. When I look back over my earlier years, I'm aghast at some of the colors I decorated my homes in, and what colors I wore, probably trying to get noticed. I probably *was* noticed all right!

In a spiritual sense, we are born squalling and shouting for attention and go on living lives wandering down the wrong roads that don't bring inner peace and joy or outer beauty. Jesus left heaven and came to earth to redeem us from our rocky paths, fill our souls with His Holy Spirit, and help us become what He dreamed of when He designed us:

> Think of yourselves the way Christ Jesus thought of himself. He had equal status with God but didn't think so much of himself that he had to cling to the advantages of that status no matter what. Not at all. When the time came, he set aside the privileges of deity and took on the status of a slave, became human! Having become human, he stayed human. It was an incredibly humbling process. He didn't claim special privileges. Instead, he lived a selfless, obedient life and then died a selfless, obedient death—and the worst kind of death at that—a crucifixion.
> Because of that obedience, God lifted him high and honored him far beyond anyone or anything, ever, so that all created beings in heaven and on earth—even those long ago dead and buried—will bow in worship before this Jesus Christ, and call out in praise that he is the Master of all, to the glorious honor of God the Father. (Philippians 2:5–11 MSG)

When I was younger, I had heard that Jesus died on the cross—but *I didn't realize He was doing it for me.* I had been somehow convinced that God didn't care for me, that I was left out. My childhood experiences of being plain and straggly left me feeling like an outsider, outside of God's care. But look at the verses above: who is really included in the above verses?

Are any created beings left out of God's plan? When I started to believe that God cared for me and wanted to help me become what He had in mind all along for me, it really excited me! He has a design for you too!

When I would do a color analysis beauty makeover, I first took off all the makeup a woman was wearing. It was nearly impossible to find which colors were her best true colors if I was matching them to a set of makeup colors that were not the real *her*. The apostle Paul wrote about the *spiritual* removing of the old self:

> Put to death, therefore, whatever belongs to your earthly nature: sexual immorality, impurity, lust, evil desires and greed, which is idolatry. Because of these, the wrath of God is coming. You used to walk in these ways, in the life you once lived. But now you must also rid yourselves of all such things as these: anger, rage, malice, slander, and filthy language from your lips. Do not lie to each other, since you have taken off your old self with its practices and have put on the new self, which is being renewed in knowledge in the image of its Creator. (Colossians 3:5-10 NIV)

These un-heavenly attitudes and actions are like the old makeup colors that we must take off before God can show His glory through us. What things do you think God wants us to take off as you look closer at St. Paul's quote above? Verse 6 is a sober reminder. What does it say to you? You may not be happy with your attitudes, and neither is God satisfied; actually, it makes Him mad. When I see in the verse above that our old, selfish actions bring God's "wrath," I don't think of a mean, mad God. I think of how we feel when our kids keep insisting on doing wrong things that will bring unhappiness—it makes us mad to watch them bring waste and unhappiness into their own lives. He has so much better in mind for us and wants to make us really happy and full of joy. Verse 7 says God knows we are all human, and we all have these evil things that we need to take off before we can get our glory makeover. Many people think that since all humans are this way, you are doomed to live this way. No, there is hope! If God tells us to rid ourselves of these things, He surely believes in us and believes that we can be changed. Furthermore, He promises to help! That's good news!

There are some "old garments" that God wants us to take off. He does not ask us to feel bad about it or beat ourselves up over it; He just asks us to stop. He would not ask us to do something that He knows we cannot do. How many negative, destructive things can you find in the above verses, and what are they? Which ones seem to dog your steps the most? Which are not particular problems for you? (Yay for our areas of strength! That makes the job a little easier!)

Read verse 10 and see that you take off the old (spiritual) makeup and clothing. Now comes the makeover. You are being renewed—that is present tense. It doesn't happen all at once when you decide to follow Christ. It is something *being* done daily. I've lived many years, and still God is patiently showing me things to put off. What image are we being made into?

God often changes a name when a heart changes. In the makeover story of Sarah in Genesis 17:15, we read that in the *before* picture, Sarah was called "Sarai," which in Hebrew means "dominator, contentious ruler." (Anyone relate to these names? What would others say about you?) Sarah mocked and refused to believe that God would give her a son in her old age, even though *Abraham had heard it from God Himself.* So first she nagged her husband into having an heir by a surrogate mother, but then demanded that he get rid of her *and* the child when trouble came. (That was the beginning of the Arabs, who have fought with the Jews ever since! See what long-reaching effects a woman can have!) However, when *she herself* heard the angel of God say she would bear a child, she became a believer. In her *after* picture,

God changed her name to "Sarah," or "noble princess." She was still a royal, but a gentler, kinder one. Abraham became so in love with her that even though she was very, very old when she died, he mourned her death deeply and refused to be comforted. When a woman becomes a heavenly woman, she isn't perfect, but those in her life are drawn to her and increasingly take her into their hearts.

I'm told that the Catholic nuns get a new name when they take their vows. *If you could choose a new name* that would describe the way you *wish* others saw you, what would it be? I don't mean names like Jane or Mary, but descriptive names, like "hopeful" or "cheerful" or "gentle." Don't think that you have to be this already—you are still in your *before* makeover picture. Just think about how you would *like* to be. What would it be? (Enjoy this!) Remember, God had a wonderful *you* in mind all along. Read again the words in Psalms 139 in the Amplified Version:

> 13 For You did form my inward parts; You did knit me together in my mother's womb.

> 14 I will confess *and* praise You *for You are fearful and wonderful and* for the awful wonder of my birth! Wonderful are Your works, and that my inner self knows right well.

> 15 My frame was not hidden from You when I was being formed in secret [and] intricately and curiously wrought [as if embroidered with various colors] in the depths of the earth [a region of darkness and mystery].

> 16 Your eyes saw my unformed substance, and in Your book all the days [of my life] were written before ever they took shape, when as yet there was none of them. (Psalm 139:13—16 Amplified Bible)

God means what he says in Psalm 139:15: *you* were "embroidered with various colors" in your mother's womb. You, personally planned and designed! I find that amazing. I always thought that I just had plain brown eyes, boring brown hair, medium beige skin. When I realized that God, *the master designer*, designed me, I looked closer. I found that although my eyes are sort of brown, they actually have many shades of green and gold and brown. My hair naturally (before the grays) was a honey-brown with some gold highlights in the sunshine! (When I started to color my gray, I went down the same road, keeping gold-honey tones.) I found that my skin was more ivory than pink, and was a good frame for my warm lip and cheek color.

Think about your colors. Look in the mirror in good light. Analyze your eyes—how many different colors do you see? What color was your hair as a young child? How has it changed, and what is your natural color now? What about your skin tone—is it pinkish, yellowish, brown, red, ivory, ebony, or somewhere in between? Think about your favorite outfit: what color is (or was) it? Do you tend to prefer clothing in neutral tones, bright vibrant primary colors, muted earth tones, soft warm colors, gentle cool colors, or classic red/navy/black colors?

God had a plan for your beauty from the very beginning, and you will be happier if you can find that plan. Pray that God will lead you to it so you can blossom into the beautiful woman he had in mind. God designed beauty all around us, and we are inspired when we are in a garden or lovely setting. Similarly, people around us will be inspired and encouraged if we are attractive. What ways can a woman practically radiate the beauty God planned?

One of my color-consultant clients had dark brown hair and dark eyes. She had medium beige skin with no cheek color or lip color. She had always felt rather plain and tended to wear neutral colors to help her disappear. She was surprised when I showed her that her palette of best colors were royal blue, true red, burgundy, and many other bold colors she never had dared to wear. I taught her to use a touch of dark raspberry lip and cheek color, and a bit of smoky gray eye shadow. When she arrived at a meeting the next week, wearing a red blouse and her new makeups, everyone was stunned. I heard someone say "Who is that beautiful model?"

Another client had medium brown hair, medium gray/green eyes, and ivory skin. She, too, felt nondescript and boring. When we tried holding up warm colors, it brought her hair, eyes and skin alive. Her best makeup colors were soft coral lips and cheeks and tawny brown eye shadow. Dressed in a peach dress, with her new makeups, she was just as delightful as a spring day.

There are so many facets to the heavenly woman makeover, and you will have some life-changing moments, as well as just plain fun times. As we begin, I know some of you might have a hard time even knowing how to begin your heavenly woman makeover, your journey into a heavenly realm. I am convinced it should start with three nice words: SORRY, THANK YOU, PLEASE—three polite words, three powerful words that can change your life. If you are confused by my earlier references to deciding to follow Christ in His heavenly ways, this makes it simple—simple enough for a child to understand. After all, Jesus said we must be like children to enter the Kingdom of Heaven:

> Unless you turn to God from your sins and become
> as little children, you will never get into the Kingdom
> of Heaven. (Matthew 18:3, The Living Bible).

Here is the Good News in a nutshell, in three simple words, which, if spoken from your heart to God, *really will* change your life:

- SORRY—"Lord, I'm SORRY I have lived my life going my own way, oblivious to Your perfect design for me, making a mess of things.
- THANK YOU for designing me, loving me enough to pay for my sins, and for coming to fix what I fouled up, making all things new in my life.

- PLEASE take my hand, fill me with Your own Holy Spirit, and make me over into a heavenly woman."

If these three words have been yours, get ready to begin your journey to become a heavenly woman!

LIVING IT:

Use a notebook to jot things down: questions you have, thoughts and experiences this week and any differences you feel. Make it a personal book that nobody else reads, and it will be interesting for you to go back and read as you grow into your beautiful new self. If you are doing this as part of a study group, you may feel like possibly sharing when the group meets next time.

Really listen to your speech, what you say, this week. Put the Colossians 3:8 filter over your mouth. Remember that God has asked you to put these things aside; ask Him for His help. Watch to see any difference in how you feel inside or how people react to you. Note it in your notebook.

Think of yourself as starting to be all new. Off with the old, on with the new, in Christ. You are becoming a "noble princess" of God: a heavenly woman! Act like it. Talk like it. Walk like it. Dress like it—dare to be beautiful, inside and outside. You are loved, by God Almighty Himself, even if by nobody else. He cares, He notices.

Start a scrapbook folder that will help you find your own style. We will add to it over the next few weeks or months and complete a project with it later on. Start now to cut out (or print) any ads or photos of women whose appearance you like. If you see a hairstyle you like, even if you don't think you could wear it, put it in. If you see a dress or outfit advertised that you really like, put it in. This is not a time to buy, but to collect a database of what you like. When you see colors you like, either in makeup, clothing, or home furnishings, cut them out and put them in. You don't have to know what your best colors or styles are yet, but start looking at what appeals to you. Pinterest boards are the way techies might do this! Or you can snap pics with your phone and save them in a Makeover Album that you can add to in your photo app on your phone. You are building your database to help you understand God's design for you. You can also accumulate your chapter notes of the Heavenly Woman book in a folder.

JUST FOR FUN:

If you have never "had your colors done," it may be easier than you thought. Get a pencil and write the A or B answers to the following questions. Think about your favorite colors, whether you prefer (A) cranberry or (B) peach, (A) blue-green or (B) yellow-green, (A) black or (B) camel, (A) snow white or (B) creamy white. If you have more A answers than B answers, you may be a cool palette: Winter (bold and clear) or Summer (softer and muted). More B answers indicate a warm palette: Autumn (muted even if vibrant) or Spring (clear and bright). You can look up color analysis online—there are several different thoughts on it. I find that Carole Jackson's original book, Color Me Beautiful is the simplest and easiest to understand. Have fun with this. Sometimes if you are really having trouble telling if you are warm or cool, it is helpful to try two blushes on: (A) cool cranberry or (B) warm peach. Your best blush will be so right for you that even if you put a lot on it doesn't look garish. However, the wrong one can look gaudy even with a minimal amount. Then look in your closet to see what color some of your favorite items are. We are sometimes surprised how often we have chosen our best colors!

Chapter 2

THE SOUGHT WOMAN:
FEELING WANTED

Well, life does go along, whether you have good communication in your marriage or not, whether you are disappointed in life or not. I learned to do laundry, somewhat, although I didn't care to do it, and, being a true child of the Sixties revolution, I resented that somehow the lot fell to me to do the laundry. I resented picking up Freddy's dirty socks from the corners of the room, and I blamed his mother for catering to him.

Also, I didn't want to come home from work and cook. I cleaned the trailer when I really had to, but I didn't know how to keep on top of it. Somehow, the whole thing was just not what I had expected. Looking back, I'm sure it wasn't what he expected, either. His mother didn't work outside the home and always had good meals on the table, kept a clean house, and somehow turned piles of laundry into neat stacks in his drawers. I was frustrated, disappointed, and not very happy. I think he wasn't either, but he was busy getting his college degree.

As time went by, we had babies, and the laundry basket was now eternally full. I'm old enough to remember the mounds of diapers in the laundry basket too, before disposable diapers changed laundry forever!

11

We had some good times, as most couples do; but overall I was not satisfied or fulfilled and didn't really know why. Where was the romantic suitor of the courting days? Where was the rose-covered cottage? Where was the *joie de vie*?

My oldest sister, who lived in Arizona, was continually sending us Christian literature, but we were thoroughly modern and saw no need for that part of yesteryear. Freddy and I made fun of it, and I threw it on the floor just to have a good laugh. One day, however, out of complete boredom, I picked up a book she had sent to me: Hannah Smith's *The Christian's Secret of a Happy Life*. I sort of thought I might learn how to refute my sister's faith, so I sat down to read it. *Surprise!* It made sense! Somehow, between the beginning and end of that book, I became a Christian! I tried to explain it to my husband, but he didn't seem to understand what had happened to me. We did go to church together, but that didn't seem to make any difference in how we got along. We didn't fight, we didn't argue. We just didn't share. The dream of an ideal marriage that we both wanted seemed to elude us.

He, unfortunately, must have felt the disappointment of our marriage in ways I didn't understand, and he was a prime target for the same thing that happens to countless couples. He started noticing other women who seemed interesting, who might be the ideal mate, someone who would make him feel important and in love again. I had no idea how to meet a man's emotional needs then, much to my regret. He worked late a lot, but I didn't think anything was amiss.

One day I took the children to the mall, and when I returned, he was gone, along with his desk, his stereo, and his clothes. *Big shock.* When he contacted me later, he said it was just because he needed space to sort out his life. I'm sure that was true, since we really didn't know how to make a marriage work.

He was confused, perhaps wondering if another woman might understand him more than I did. That is a real danger for a man, if he feels lonely in the marriage. I was the last to know. A divorced woman in the church called me one day and said, "I don't want you to hear it from someone else. I have been seeing your husband. I'm sorry, but we are in love." I was so surprised that I actually thought she was joking with me. But she wasn't.

So, now the *biggest shock of all*, and the greatest disappointment of life, had hit me between the eyes. I felt rejected, left behind, unwanted. The pain was excruciating, above anything I had thought possible. The only guy I had ever seriously dated since I was 15, the one I had given my life to, had left me for another. *And* he had left me with three small children. I had worked low-level jobs to put him through college, but once the children were born, I had not worked. I had no career and had no idea what I would do. In the midst of pain, I took on the victim's role, and felt bitter, blaming him for it all. (Only years later would I realize my part in the breakdown of the relationship.)

We all want desperately to be wanted. To be unwanted is the saddest thing of all, and that is what is so excruciating, whether we are in what feels like a loveless marriage, or whether we are actually left behind. I cried, I nearly died. I wondered how people survived those things.

The church family was a great support for me during that time. (Freddy left the church, quite understandably, since outwardly it looked like he was the villain; nobody really knows what pain he was going through trying to make sense of his life.) In my despair, I really turned to God at a level I had never done. I discovered that if I read the Psalms out loud to God—sometimes crying them, sometimes praying them, being totally honest with God, pouring out whatever I felt—I found that He was always there, always met me, always understood.

God showed me some painful things about myself over those sad months. I saw my selfishness, my unrealistic expectations; yet He let me know He loved me anyway. I cried tears of joy at His grace and forgiveness. I had lots of adjustments to make, as my role of wife and stay-at-home mom was suddenly gone. I was no longer sought by my husband; I felt rejected. He had chosen another, and I was left behind.

Fears and insecurities from my past flooded back and added to my desperation. One of my earliest memories was when I was not even 3 years old. We—Mom, Daddy, and three older sisters— were on a trip "out West," a laborious journey in an old car and camper trailer, all the way from Pennsylvania to California. That was back in the days before freeways or air-conditioned cars, so it was a long, hard journey across mountains and deserts. Times were hard in the coal mining country of Pennsylvania in the 1940s, and Daddy was looking for work.

We arrived at my uncle's home in California, bedraggled, poor, and hot. For the first time, I saw my little cousin Carole Lee, who was four, and the picture of her yet lives many years later in my head, defining beauty, defining me. Her hair was honey gold ringlets tied back with a pink ribbon, and she wore a pink ruffled dress, patent leather shoes, and snowy white socks with lace. *Lace!* I had never seen such a vision. It was like seeing into heaven. It was awakening something new in me, even at that tender age, that there was such a thing as beauty. But I still feel the seeping awareness, the reddening of the face, as I realized that I was wearing only underpants and I was barefoot, and my hair was stringy and brown. People think little children aren't capable of such thoughts, but I know what happened to me, and how hard it is to erase and replace them. (As an adult, I can see that probably my twenty-something mother with 4 little girls, having just survived a harrowing trip across the desert without air conditioning and with little money, might have been just too overwhelmed to even think of freshly pressed dresses for her girls.)

But memory burns deep, and silently forms our inner image. That shabby, embarrassed tiny girl lived in my skin from then on, telling me that though God made others pretty, I was not included in that group. Could there be a fair God? He cared for others, but I felt forgotten. Unwashed. Unwanted by God. Not chosen. Many years I felt unhappy with what God had given me, discontent with my hair, my thinness, my looks, my personality; that was, until Freddy, the "football star," courted me. *Me! Chosen! Preferred over those pretty cheerleaders!* But now he was gone with another, and the devastation returned, crushing me. I so wanted to be chosen.

It is amazing to look back and see how the old Garden of Eden story replays in our lives. Adam and Eve, though having been given the abundance of the garden, focused not on what *was* given, but on what was *not* given. The entire abundance of the garden was theirs, and only one tree was off limits. It was Satan himself who whispered, "God doesn't care. God is withholding from you." Satan always grasps for more power over us, and like Snow White's stepmother, always gives us a poison apple. He blinds us to the good, if he can. He wants to take our focus off the blessings we have and needle us with what we don't have. My parents loved me and actually provided a sort of Eden farm life, with fun and pets and work and laughter. I should have enjoyed a healthy, complete self-image, but very early I heard the accusing voice of the devil, and I believed him. Even my nickname made me cringe: "Squeaky." Not Dolly or Cutie or Punkin, but Squeaky, for my thin little voice. Like my thin little hair.

It didn't help that my golden-ringleted sister had sparkly blue eyes, pink cheeks, and sang like a little bird. But doesn't it make you laugh at God's ways? Here I am, many years later, and God has finally convinced me that I am not forgotten after all, showing me that I am *chosen! Even me!*

God used the hard time after Freddy left, where I felt the pain of being *un-chosen* so devastatingly, to start to re-program my inner life. I *was* chosen! God has chosen those that the world didn't choose! Little Squeaky in my head had to move over as I read:

> You have not chosen me, but I have chosen you!
> (John 15:16 KJV)
> I have chosen you out of the world. (John 15:19 KJV)
> God has chosen the weak and foolish. (1 Cor 1:27 KJV)
> You are chosen and precious. (1 Peter 2:4 KJV)
> You are a chosen generation, a royal priesthood! (1
> Peter 2:9 KJV)

Years of being the clumsy one chosen last for a team in gym class, and of being a shy wallflower at school dances, had added to my already poor self-image. As I started to embrace the wonder that God has actually chosen me, I realized that partly I had said "yes" to my first marriage proposal because I was feeling chosen—that was heady stuff. But now *that* marriage offer was taken back, and my role was all up-side-down. God had a big job ahead to remodel me and my life, but He was starting.

It may sound old fashioned, but I think that in our heart of hearts, we women really still want our man to beat a path to our door, to bring us flowers, to ask us out. From the first time we are interested in a man, we dress to attract his attention, in hopes he will choose us. We want the man to be the knight in shining armor who comes on a white horse, adoring us and laying his life down for us. The man is naturally the suitor; the woman wants to be wooed. Even after the wedding, as everyday life sets in, we want our man to seek us out for company, for companionship, for love. If he doesn't, which happens a lot of the time, we can feel unappreciated, unloved, unfulfilled, unhappy. He may love us, but in his mind assumes that if he provides for us and treats us decently, it will be enough. Our unhappiness and lack of appreciation of his work can frustrate him.

Really, truly, we want to be sought. Our eye can stray to another man who we think will be different. If we allow it, *he* will seek us, pay attention to our thoughts and ideas, and want to please us—during the wooing stage. We can think that everyday life with this new person will be our dream; but now many years of experience in ministry and counseling office shows us that the dream most often becomes a nightmare. Once the home is broken up and the children wounded, life with Mr. Next, after all, is not the constant courtship we expected. Women today struggle with this more than in past generations, since divorce has lost its stigma in society and is easier to get. Women today don't feel "stuck" like our grandmothers might have during a "bad patch." The alarming rate of marriage breakups has resulted in not happier marriages but often bigger regrets. We can miss the good life because we don't understand the stages of courtship and marriage, and we *can look in the wrong places to be sought.*

We want our man to worship the ground we walk on, and we want to revere and worship him. But how to get to that point? There are many things a wise woman can do to encourage her man to be all he can be, and we will look at many of them in our heavenly woman study. But even if her man does not seem to want more in the relationship, and her heart aches by feeling unwanted, there is good news. No, not *good*—WONDERFUL news!

The wonderful news for us women is that *we are sought* for a personal and intimate relationship—*by the most important and most powerful person of all, the God of the universe.* Down through the centuries, great people have found incredible joy and fulfillment from their relationship with God. God the Father is *seeking* people for a close, worshipful relationship. He sought me. He is seeking *you.* He wants *you.*

> It's who you are and the way you live that count
> before God. Your worship must engage your spirit
> in the pursuit of truth. That's the kind of people the
> Father is out looking for: those who are simply and

> honestly *themselves* before him in their worship. God is sheer being itself—Spirit. Those who worship him must do it out of their very being, their spirits, their true selves, in adoration. (John 4:24, The Message)

Do you see what is God *seeking* from you, that you alone have the power to give Him? The key to having this need of being sought and wanted in our lives fulfilled is to turn to God and say to him, "Thank you for wanting me! I want you; I want to worship you in Spirit and in truth, whatever that means. Show me." We have tried to find fulfillment in our marriages, our work, or children. But all fall short. God alone can bring us this joy, and once we experience it, and are changed by it, we will be full to overflowing with contentment. We can be happy in situations that would have been impossible before.

It is an amazing story we find in John 4, leading up to the verse we read above. A woman is busy about her life and her work. She has had five husbands, but has a live-in now. She is not a religious woman, and is surprised when Jesus breaks into her day, asking her for something He needs: a drink of water. She doesn't understand who he is, or why he is there, but he whets *her* thirst by telling her that he can give her something in her life that will really satisfy her needs, forever: "living water." She is shocked, and says, "Then give me this living water, so I will never thirst again." They get into a discussion of her life, and he prophetically tells her that he knows about her messed-up love life. *The woman had just wanted to be loved, to be sought after.* Disappointed by five men, she was hoping that this sixth one would really fill her need for being sought after. She is really surprised that the Kingdom of God has crashed into her life; she wasn't even looking for it, didn't know she needed it. Often we don't know we need it either.

> A woman, a Samaritan, came to draw water. Jesus
> said, "Would you give me a drink of water?" (His
> disciples had gone to the village to buy food for
> lunch.) (John 4:7 MSG)

Jesus asks her for H_2O—actual water—that she has in her
pitcher. It is something she can give, something he needs. I find
it amazing that Jesus, creator of the universe, has a need that a
mere human, I, Squeaky, can meet! The woman was confused
when Jesus talked to her about worship, so He told her what
he had told *nobody* before, that He was indeed the promised
Messiah, the Son of God:

> The woman said, "I don't know about that [where
> to worship]. I do know that the Messiah is coming.
> When he arrives, we'll get the whole story."
>
> "I am he," said Jesus. "You don't have to wait any
> longer or look any further." (John 4:25,26 MSG)

The woman at the well was busy with her life, and was
surprised by the Son of God while she was getting supper. Or at
least getting water for supper. He comes into our life at just the
right moment, but when least expected. Jesus crashed into my
life, like Super Man, coming just at the right time to save me
from my despair. Is it possible that you are here because God has
crashed into your life, seeking a relationship with you, either for
the first time, or desiring a deeper relationship with you? How
do you feel about the God of the Universe desiring to be part of
your everyday life, desiring to give you a beauty make-over from
the inside out?

Jesus is the one who knows all things, not just about the
woman with five husbands and one live-in, but about you and me.
It can affect your relationships with husband, children, relatives,
neighbors, co-workers, etc., because He knows all about your

longings and disappointments. And He, who knows all, promises to guide us through our troubled waters!

> So be content with who you are, and don't put on airs. God's strong hand is on you; he'll promote you at the right time. Live carefree before God; he is most careful with you. (1 Peter 5:6,7 MSG)

> ...casting all your anxiety on him, because he cares about you. (1 Peter 5:7 NASB)

When we don't argue back to those who we feel mistreat us, but instead humble ourselves and "cast our anxieties on God," He will give us great peace inside, and others will see a different person. They may be surprised. We see the beginnings of being remade into a new woman. A glimpse of an amazing woman. A potential heavenly woman!

Probably we all have already asked for the "living water" from Jesus as our *savior* sometime in our lives, perhaps as children in Sunday School, and if asked we would say we are Christians. However, it can be better than that! Jesus offers *us* living water for our own unique problems. As we deal with hard situations or events, we can quietly and inwardly turn to Jesus and ask for living water for that situation, right on the spot! Religious people call that prayer. But it is just Jesus whispering to us, "I can help. I care for you. Don't worry," and us responding to Him, thanking him and "making our requests to him."

> Don't fret or worry. Instead of worrying, pray. Let petitions and praises shape your worries into prayers, letting God know your concerns. Before you know it, a sense of God's wholeness, everything coming together for good, will come and settle you down. It's wonderful what happens when Christ displaces worry at the center of your life. (Philippians 4:6,7, MSG)

Jesus knows that the world around us is busy going about their miserable existence, full of disappointments, and that they won't *believe* unless they see something supernatural. *He is willing to break into their lives and show them, prophetically, that there is more, that life can be better!* After he broke into the woman-at-the-well's life, she went to her friends and became an ambassador for God, a heavenly woman! People knew she wasn't a religious woman, and they knew how many husbands she had had—so God was able to show people around her that He can use anyone to be His daughter and His ambassador! Is it possible that God is breaking into our lives so that others may see a new spiritual dimension through our lives? If others are disappointed in life, and they see *living water* in our lives, won't it make them thirsty for God? Will our mates be surprised if we are joyful and forgiving? (Probably they won't trust that it is true at first!)

LIVING IT:

Living Water! Author Esther Burrows tells us that God is seeking those who will come to him for the Living Water. (Read her book *Splash the Living Water: Turning Daily Interruptions into Life-giving Encounters.)* Living Water can be soft responses instead of anger or demands. Living Water can be acting and reacting in unexpectedly kind ways. People might be surprised. They may wonder what's gotten into you. Ask God to show you ways to "splash" Living Water into your situations and let it splash onto others. Make notes in your notebook about what Living Water might look like in your life. Look for minutes in your week where the gentle voice of God whispers, "Here's a chance for Living Water!" (Share what happens when they gather next week, if you are in a study group.)

Tracking your makeover. Continue writing any thoughts in your notebook. What spoke to you in this chapter? Any questions come to mind about the scriptures in this chapter?

Who are you, really? Keep looking for items that you love in magazines, online, wherever. If you can cut the page out or print it, put it in your folder. Or just save it on your computer in a file "Heavenly Me." On your smartphone, you can save it to your "Notes" (or the free "Evernote" app that syncs perfectly with your computer if you download Evernote there too.) Wherever you save it, it is going to help you define your own uniqueness.

FOR FUN

Last week we looked at putting off the old and putting on the new. Marie Kondo says keep what "sparks joy" in you. Why not bless others with things that are good but don't really add to your joy? You might just make someone's day. Are there things around you that you really just clean or move around but they don't add to your joy? Once you start doing this, it can be addictive! And fun!

Chapter 3

THE SEEKING WOMAN: LOOKING HEAVENWARD

So my journey began—my journey out of rejection, despair, and unrealistic expectations. I looked into the Bible, and things became clearer. I cried out to God, desperately, and He began to show me some things that a Christian woman, a wife, should do. I say began, because it has been a long process. I changed my expectations from always wanting a husband to meet all my needs to reaching out to God for my happiness, my satisfaction in life. I saw that life was not a fairy story, not an endless romance novel. I knew I was going to have to relearn some things, from the simple things like how to do laundry and run a responsible household, to the more complicated things like learning to be unselfish, kind, and gentle. It appeared that it was too late for my marriage, but I was determined to become a better person.

A change happened as I started to seek a more heavenly way. Instead of trying to be a better person in order to save my marriage, I wanted to be a better person to please God, and to bring a touch of Heaven to those around me. I Peter 3, the part about being a peaceful and gentle person, became my ideal—the scripture mirror I looked into as I started on a heavenly makeover journey.

> Rather, [your beauty] should be that of your inner
> self, the unfading beauty of a gentle and quiet spirit,
> which is of great worth in God's sight. For this is the
> way the holy women of the past who put their hope
> in God used to adorn themselves. (I Peter 3:4,5 NIV)

Amazingly, Freddy's greener pastures didn't look too green to him once he was over the fence. Evidently, the grass wasn't really greener over there! You've heard about the "everyday life problem," haven't you? The excitement of courtship fades when marriage becomes a daily routine. Then they remarry, and soon that becomes the "everyday life" so he or she must go out looking again. It goes on and on. At Christmas time, Freddy came to visit and said he had made a mistake, that he missed us, and wanted to come back home. He was the suitor again, calling and bringing gifts and begging for forgiveness. I gladly took him back, glad for the second chance to show him that I was determined to change into a Christian wife much different from the old me.

I read mountains of books about how to be the perfect wife, how to keep house, how to keep up with laundry, how to cook, how to dress, how to improve. I was determined to be the best wife this time.

We joined an active church nearby, and I thought we had a real chance to reclaim the marriage. I spent time early every morning after I got Freddy off to work, before the children awakened, reading the Bible and praying, and my joy was springing up from my heart. Now I wasn't trying to get my sense of peace and happiness from my husband, not nagging for attention or demanding things to be my way.

The damage we had done over the years and infidelity had taken its toll on our relationship, but I was trusting God to mend us. I read everything from the dizzy fun of *The Total Woman* to the staid goodness of Edith Schaeffer's *The Hidden Art of Homemaking*. Marabel Morgan published *The Total Woman* in

1973, sold over 500,000 copies in the first year, and it was the most successful non-fiction book in America in 1974! My girlfriends at church were all on board to improve their marriages too, and our Bible study group became a fellowship of the *new women*. I think the era of the 70's was a special season of "home improvement" for Christian wives.

One funny thing happened to my sister Joanne that gives you an idea of the lengths we were going to after reading *The Total Woman*. She read that to make her man feel important, and to make sure he felt his needs were paramount in her life, she should think of creative and wonderful ways to welcome him home from work. Imagine this: her husband arrived home to find a tablecloth spread on the living room floor with an elegant picnic spread out on it, and his wife perfumed and dressed to impress. In the bedroom, just over the head of the bed, she had a hung a new elaborate metal scroll-work wall decor with many votive candles burning on it. So romantic! The candlelight made a beautiful and ambient glow that lured them into the bedroom as they finished their picnic. Her husband was really surprised by it all, but nothing could compare to his surprise when his head bumped the whole candle-lit thing off the wall, and molten wax and fire flew all over the bed.

We had lots of fun sharing our experiences in the Bible study group as we passed our books and ideas around. I can only imagine what the husbands thought, or what their discussions might have been like if they were meeting as a men's group (which they didn't). They might have wished we would just go back to being religious! We did such things as memorizing sports facts and insisting on sitting next to husbands during every TV sports program, and trying to converse on all things sports. One of the gals made reservations at a restaurant and hotel, and "kidnapped" her husband at work, after leaving the kids at her mom's, and actually blindfolded him as she drove him to their destination.

There were some really silly things we did—but we were seriously trying to do the hard unseen stuff too, "setting our minds on things above," above the fray, so to speak. Many of us had realized that we had let our marriages grow weeds, and we were determined to make gardens out of the tangles.

I tried to learn the art of biting my tongue, and attempted to learn the foreign tongue of sports, memorizing (some of) the names and numbers of football players. I didn't do it well, I'm sure, but I did try. I sat up late to keep hubby company until my eyes nearly crossed, and got up in the wee hours with my toddler who never slept through the night, and I got up early to get him off to work with a breakfast (sometimes—but sometimes I failed), and later to get the others off to school. I tried to not be so religious that it would turn him off. I thought things would have to improve between us, even though we still didn't share much except the popcorn in front of the television.

But then one Saturday morning we were just resting in bed, before the kids woke up, as the sun shone in the patio door of our bedroom that led to a private deck. The birds were singing, and it promised to be a fine day. I was thinking of what fun we could have on such a bright, warm day, and was chatting about it. Freddy was acting a little odd and quiet. "What's wrong?" I asked, and he wouldn't say anything. My heart started to sink in premonition, but I could still hardly believe it when he finally blurted out that he felt like a heel, that he had been seeing someone and needed help to avoid going down the road he had before. He actually groaned, and said my changing had made him ashamed that he had started seeing someone again. He said he wanted to get counseling and try to save our marriage. He picked up the phone and called our pastor right then, who said to come right over.

My new Super-Christian-Wife world was shattered and lay in jagged pieces all over the room. It seemed like the clock and my heart both stopped as I lay there on the bed in our beautiful bedroom, the streaming sunshine suddenly seeming all wrong for this setting. Shattered is the best word to describe it all. The first unrealistic world of our early marriage had been shattered because it was all wrong and needed changed from the ground up. This one was shattered, but I didn't know why. Hadn't I been doing the work, seeking God, making changes?

So we gathered up the shards of our marriage and went for pastoral marriage counseling. We continued for about 6 months, and I thought that at last, with help, we could put things together and make it. I felt pretty confused, because the pastor said I needed to quit being a Christian so much and just try to make my husband happy. I thought I was doing that, but evidently I was going about it all wrong. He told me to quit reading the Bible, and he said if I came to his house while my kids were at school and helped his wife clean and cook, maybe I would learn something about how to be a good wife. So three days a week, I took the older kids to school and took the toddler to the pastor's house, and was like a servant. I cleaned their bathroom, helped cook and serve for their social events. Looking back, I am amazed that I thought that was the right thing to do. But I wanted to save the marriage, and the one we trusted to know how to fix things prescribed it.

I worked hard helping the pastor's wife and taking care of my home and family. I got pregnant with our fourth child, and was thrilled. We moved into a brand new large home. I was getting little sleep and wasn't feeling as good with this pregnancy as the first three. One day, we were at a social function when I was about 7 months along, and I started to feel really crampy. Freddy took me to the hospital, and they gave me something to slow down and stop the contractions, as it was way too early for a delivery. The next day I came home but had to have bed rest for a while. Freddy had an important job downtown, and couldn't stay home more than a day or two, so our twelve-year-old son fixed a lot of peanut butter sandwiches for meals. He was going to get good at that.

I recovered, and the pregnancy was saved, but somehow our marriage wasn't. I could see Freddy drifting away a bit. We didn't go to counseling anymore. Before the baby was born, he was working later and later, and often overnight.

In the hospital after our baby boy was born, I really got the new-baby blues, afraid that the baby's dad would be leaving us for good when a decent amount of time passed. You can bet that I really worked hard at being the 100 percent perfect wife when I got home from the hospital, and I did think maybe I could keep him from leaving. He stayed with us longer than I thought he might, but more and more he was "out" until late, doing "extra projects" at work. He was never at his office if I called, and I soon realized that he wasn't actually working late. I don't know what anguish and confusion he was going through, but it must have been great, because even though he loved the children, he was being drawn away from the home.

One night when the baby was about a year and a half old, I lay in the bed crying, as I suspected that Freddy was not really working late. At about 2 a.m., something odd happened. Other nights I would lie there just waiting for the sound of the tires on the gravel and feel relieved when he finally came home. This time, it was odd. I just quit crying. It was like the crying was over, and I realized that I didn't *want* to hear the sound of the gravel. *Ever again.* This time, I had the feeling that it was really over. I think God was preparing me emotionally for the end of the marriage. God never wants a marriage to end, but He does let us make choices.

Maybe if I had known from the beginning of my first marriage what I know now, the marriage could have been saved. I don't know. I don't know why he was so mixed up, but he finally flat out told me that he just didn't want me and didn't want a family. Maybe he was having a midlife crisis. Maybe he wanted his marriage *and* his freedom, I don't know. All I knew was I was done. The marriage was done.

You may be in a difficult relationship right now, and you might pour your whole heart into saving it, yet still lose it because either the other one refuses to be won back, or you are unwilling to wait it out in hope it will change. But know this: God is faithful: seek Him, and He will meet you and deliver you—either deliver you *in* the relationship, or deliver you *from* it. Only He knows. Perhaps you can take comfort from the scripture in 1 Corinthians 7:15. It came to me this way: I had been in turmoil for years trying to keep my man in the marriage. I had beaten myself up over it, tried to change myself, agonized over it all the time, and there was no peace about it in my life. One day, after Freddy left for the last time, I was reading the Bible and came to this verse: "if he wants to leave, let him leave...God has called us to peace." *WOW. Peace.* Wouldn't it be wonderful to have peace!

One of the great things God told me I'll never forget. It was when I had tried my best to save my marriage, but lost it anyway, and I felt that I was a failure. I was standing at my kitchen sink, tears streaming down my face and water streaming down my wrists. It was almost as if God spoke in a real voice. I suppose it was in my heart, but it seemed as though the sound was echoing in the room. God asked me, "Was I a failure of a God, because the Israelites left me, again and again?" He reminded me that Israel had deserted Him many times, in spite of all He had provided for them. I was really released by that, and praise Him to this day for taking the time to reassure me that the failure was not because I was a poor wife. In fact, even though I had been left behind again, I had learned a lot about God's plans for Christian wives and women, and I had learned where my real happiness came from. I might have been left behind like an outdated model car by the man in my life, but God loved me and was seeking to comfort me and assure me that I was His, and He would never leave me.

It is wonderful to find, as we did last week, that God is seeking us; that he wants a close relationship with those who are seeking him. That is the beginning of the (inner) beauty makeover we are hoping for over the next few months as we travel together in a quest to become heavenly women. Although a lot of our study mentions husbands, a heavenly woman is heavenly for *everyone* around her, and is no different whether she is single or married. She can add a touch of the divine to every place she goes, to every life she touches. *Perhaps I had to lose a marriage to learn this.* There is so much more to us women than a marriage. Whether married or single, we have a home; we have a life. We are women, women of God. We are uniquely feminine, whether we are married or not. I still needed to find how to be that feminine woman, on her own. Now not part of a pair, nor just the feminine half of a couple: just feminine. God's daughter, loved and full of grace and beauty.

Colossians 3:1 tells us to "keep on seeking the things above, where Christ is;" then God repeats it again in the very next verse, "Set your mind on the things above, not on the things of the earth." God knows that we women, especially, like the earthly things that bring delight to the eye and senses. Woman, more than man, loves pretty things, things that please the eye. Woman likes fragrances. She has the nesting instinct to make a home pretty. She tends to want soft fabrics and flowers and candles.

It is natural to like the earthly things, in addition to the heavenly things. It is good to make a pretty, comforting home and to make a great marriage. However, it is in "setting our minds on" *them* that is wrong, for everything in life is temporary. If we set our minds on heavenly things, our joy and happiness doesn't fall apart when life changes on us; but as women, let us sprinkle our woman's magic on as much around us as we can!

She maketh herself coverings of tapestry; her clothing is silk and purple. (Proverbs 31:22 KV21)

The word "coverings" is one used in the Bible for furniture coverings, like throws or slipcovers. Proverbs 31 gives lots of encouragement in ways we can be a heavenly woman, a woman who makes her home pretty, comfortable, and welcoming. If, however, the home becomes more important than the family living there, and everyone is afraid to touch anything, the woman crosses the line from being smart about making a cozy home to "setting her mind" on the earthly things of the house.

I have never yet met a woman who delighted when her husband strayed. Have you? I know that in my life it was terrible. If there are ways, feminine ways, that help put yourself in your husband's affectionate thoughts, wouldn't you be wise to put some effort into those ways? What about grown sons—if they view you as soft and feminine and vulnerable, do you think they would be more likely to check on you, bring you firewood, gifts, or visit? If you are domineering and demanding and sulky, are they perhaps less likely to visit you?

It's ok to be smart about being very feminine. A perfume ad said, "Be a mind-sticker" and showed a man dreaming of a woman wearing the fragrance he couldn't forget. The heavenly woman tries to be a mind-sticker. Not just with perfume, although that is a good beginning, but by doing things and providing things that will cause your mister to go a little misty thinking of you and of home while he is out in the world. If you are alone, and others in your life think of you and your home in a friendly and sentimental way, wouldn't they be more likely to visit? Wouldn't relationships blossom? Wouldn't loneliness fade? Wouldn't your home look like a safe place for those in your life who are hurting? Wouldn't others start to view you as a heavenly woman? As we become heavenly women, the home can be a little bit of heaven for the weary travelers of our households and beyond.

Acknowledging a woman's connection to the five senses, now focus on heavenly things. Reach higher. Reach heavenward.

So, even though there are many things we can do in the

natural realm to make our homes warm and cozy and ourselves beautiful, we must recognize that we will live better in the earthly realm if we first set our minds on heavenly things. *Keep seeking* the things of God, and you will find that all the rest will be enhanced. As this study progresses over the weeks, and as we become transformed more and more into heavenly women, we will look at some of the earthly things as well. But first, the things above. The heavenly unseen realm is the *true* realm, where you find true values, eternal things. This *seen* world is passing away. It is temporary.

The Bible says "keep on" seeking the things above. But what happens when we set our minds to seek God's ways, and then our husband or our child or our boss or our neighbor does something that really gets to us? The "things above" is the hardest realm, because it is the unseen realm. It can't be touched by the 5 senses. It transcends our natural womanly skills. Satan, the "god of this world" (2 Corinthians 4:4), wants us to be blinded to the unseen realm, but *God wants us to seek it:*

> In whom the god of this world hath blinded the minds of them which believe not, lest the light of the glorious gospel of Christ, who is the image of God, should shine unto them. (2 Corinthians 4:4 BRG)

In 2 Corinthians 4:18, the word "seen" in the Greek is "blepo," which means to behold, to heed, to be aware of, not just using our eyeballs!

> While we look not at the things which are seen, but at the things which are not seen: for the things which are seen are temporal; but the things which are not seen are eternal. (2 Corinthians 4:18 KJ21)

In the beginning, Satan lied to Eve. He said "Ha. Has God really said....?" and he appealed to her senses, and she saw that the fruit delighted her eyes. She was tempted and ate some of it. God had wanted her to trust him in the unseen realm that the fruit was not good for her, *because He said so.* Satan still wants to trap woman into thinking that the *seen* realm is the one to go for, and that God doesn't really mean what he says in the Bible. If Satan can get us to doubt that God really knows what is good for us, then we strike out on our own; we try to get our way in the world, thinking we know what is best for us. Just like the fruit Satan offered, our own earthly desires will get us off on our own and away from God's ways. The fruit looks good, but rots quickly.

When the woman saw that the tree looked like good eating and realized what she would get out of it—she'd know everything!—she took and ate the fruit and then gave some to her husband, and he ate.

> Immediately the two of them did "see what's really going on"—saw themselves naked! They sewed fig leaves together as makeshift clothes for themselves. (Genesis 3:6,7 MSG)

Often we women are told that we can't have something our way, yet we see it and want it. If we go after it, even knowing it isn't God's will, we usually get much more than we bargained for. It doesn't just affect ourselves; it reaches into our homes and into the lives of others. What awesome and possibly terrifying power a woman has over those in her home and her sphere! We do need to seriously "seek the things above," and make sure we are heading in the heavenly direction. Look at the power given to a woman about her home:

> Every wise woman builds her household, but a foolish woman tears it down with her own hands. (Proverbs 14:1 AMPC)

Not only is a woman powerful, her *attitude* in the home is very contagious. If she is crabby, everyone pays. If she is cheerful, everyone feels better. It may not seem fair to have so much depend on the woman, but it is actually an honor to have that much "power" entrusted to us. When things seem to have gone all wrong, and we are tempted to upset the household, God reminds us of His perspective:

> So if you're serious about living this new resurrection life with Christ, *act* like it. Pursue the things over which Christ presides. Don't shuffle along, eyes to the ground, absorbed with the things right in front of you. Look up, and be alert to what is going on around Christ—that's where the action is. See things from his perspective. (Colossians 3:1,2 MSG)

When things get stressful or chaotic around the house or office, we can take a quick trip inside our hearts to the heavenly realm, where Jesus is. He is there, waiting for us to seek him, to ask for His Spirit to fill us, and He will fill us with peace. Learning this is like moving up to the next level of your heavenly beauty makeover!

When we have a bad day, and we are disappointed, we need to remind ourselves that our inner person is hidden in a secret place with God, in a place where we are loved and cherished, and where we are being made beautiful. And nobody can take that away from us:

> Your new life, which is your real life—even though invisible to spectators—is with Christ in God. He is your life. When Christ (your real life, remember) shows up again on this earth, you'll show up, too— the real you, the glorious you. Meanwhile, be content with obscurity, like Christ. (Colossians 3:3,4 MSG)

God keeps seeking us, keeps reminding us, "Seek the things

above...." The *true* woman keeps seeking the heavenly realm, the true realm, the unseen realm of God's world around us. That is the secret to peace and beauty within.

LIVING IT:

Keep up the LIVING IT from Chapters 1 & 2—it takes time to form new habits, so keep it in mind. We are adding to our inner beauty makeover kit.

This week, look for glimpses into God's unseen realm. When things get hectic, or when others are unkind or unfair to you, or you can't get your way in this "seen" realm, look beyond it into God's "unseen" realm. Ask Him to fill you with His Spirit, so you have peace in the storm, and grace to be kind and loving. Make notes in your notebook about your progress. If you are in a group study, next week share how it influenced your week.

FOR FUN:

Making your home a cozy, comfortable and easy place to be should be fun. One thing that is really satisfying is to organize clothing drawers, and it will eliminate lots of frustration for yourself and for your family. Do the Marie Kondo way of stacking things *vertically*, and you will never go back to having to dig through layers of shirts, jeans, etc. You can look up Marie on YouTube, "Tidying Up," to see how to fold this revolutionary way. She has written *The Life-changing Magic of Tidying Up*, which you would really enjoy! Once you have the clothing reorganized, you will want to do your kitchen towel drawer, bath shelves, etc. You are taking back your home, bringing order, making even little hidden corners heavenly! There is no stopping us now!

Chapter 4

THE FEMININE WOMAN: GENTLE PROTECTOR AND HELPER

Now I was alone. Well, as alone as a single mom with four kids can be. I was feeling lost and scared. I was awarded the house in the divorce, but no cash reserves to meet the large mortgage. Freddy said we had none, and he, being a professional accountant, had always done all our household books, so I really had no idea. He was just naturally one who liked to keep track of figures, and I had happily left it to him. The child support and alimony at the time were minimal; enough to just barely get by, if we were very economical. I had a new appreciation for how hard single moms had it.

I felt the need to protect my children not only from the pain of the family falling apart, but suddenly also from the wolf at the door. I hadn't worked since the children were born; our agreement had been that I would work on my degree of PHT (Put Hubby Through) so he could pursue his college degree full time, and then later I would be the full-time mom and he would be the bread-winner. Now that plan was gone, and I had no idea what to do. Child care for four children would be more costly than any job I might get would provide. I just couldn't bear to leave the baby with strangers in daycare. He was still cute and round and only saying "Tikky" (his stuffed kitty)—such separation trauma would only add to that of his daddy leaving! I couldn't explain to a baby why I would abandon him to strangers all day. No, there had to be another way. I turned to my new best Friend, Jesus, and asked for guidance.

It wasn't long before a nearby church was planning a women's seminar, and they had heard that I had been "doing colors" for some of the women in the church, and asked me if I would give them a demonstration. Sure, I could use some fun in my life, and colors were fun. During the previous year, one of the myriad books on self-improvement I devoured was *Color Me Beautiful*, by Carole Jackson. I've been an amateur artist since I was young, and the color theories she suggested fascinated me. I discovered I had a talent for "color analysis," finding the best clothing and makeup colors for a woman's unique complexion.

The seminar was such a success that I found I had a list of women who were willing to pay for a color analysis. Aha! God showed me that I could do something to earn money and not leave the children. I started looking for colors in fabric stores, buying just quarter-yard pieces, to build a bank of color shade drapes to hold up to faces, eyes, and hair. I turned my dining room into a color studio and hung pretty draperies across the doorways to hide the kitchen and family room. Thankfully, the dining room was off an impressive two-story entry foyer, so it lent a bit of professionalism as clients entered. (What they didn't know was that there were four little kids upstairs, playing in their bedrooms while I had a client—and that I paid them a dollar each if I didn't hear any noises!) God was helping me all the way. Many times I would silently pray while holding up colors, asking God to show me which to choose. Sometimes it was really hard to decide, but as I prayed, suddenly I could see it. I could see the palette for each client, and the gals left with a new sense of their own special beauty. The gals were thrilled, and I was very very grateful.

A cable TV show invited me to come and demonstrate my colors, and word got around in the area about this exciting new thing. Soon I was asked to address whole ballrooms of saleswomen for cosmetic company conventions, and many of those attending made appointments to have their "colors done." Although I wasn't making bags of money, I was at last able to pay bills and was gaining some self respect and confidence that I could make it alone. It helped me to heal from the crack in my world and helped me to feel like a whole person—not half a couple. I felt that my little brood was safe, and that God would help me to protect them.

I had lots of time to read the Bible and learn from God during those days and long evenings. Although I should have been soured on the whole idea of marriage, I found it fascinating to discover what a Christian marriage should really mean. It was sobering, too, to see areas where I had missed it even though I had tried hard to learn and make changes. It was too late to go back and fix them, but it helped to understand, and it helped me to quit playing the "blame game," either towards my ex or inwardly towards myself.

In all the ancient religions and in all the old Bible times, there were few women's rights—not even to fidelity from her husband. But Christianity alone gives marriage sanctity and a wonderful significance where the wife as well as the husband has claim to the perfect fidelity of the mate. With the birth of Christianity, the wife ceased to be merely a helper of her husband, but something infinitely more. Her feminine contribution to marriage is elevated from merely sex, procreation, and housekeeping (as in some religions) to an equal but different companion for the male. This is true femininity, godly femininity! But it differs from the world's view, different from what I had thought. My mixed-up life had teetered between the "stuff it down" doormat idea and the demands for things my way. My ex didn't understand it any more than I did. Oh, if only we had both gotten on board with the Biblical idea of marriage years ago!

> You husbands in the same way, live with your wives in an understanding way, as with someone weaker, since she is a woman; and show her honor as a fellow heir of the grace of life, so that your prayers will not be hindered. (1 Peter 3:7 NASB)

A Christian wife, no longer just a helper in the *natural realm* in the here and now, is half a partnership in *eternal life!* The wife is an heir to the grace of life. The word "fellow" usually means shared, equal partners. Of all the religions in the world, Christianity stands out in giving women true equality. Yet, once we start trying to fit into God's plan, we see that this equality has different facets. We are truly feminine, unique.

The beginning of the verse is a little bothersome, where Peter refers to women as "weaker vessels." The term *weak* is one of those that in our culture is a "fighting word" for women, isn't it? We want to say, "Weak in what way? Don't we do it all? Work, bear babies, raise kids, get up in the night with kids, dress and feed them, do the shopping, trip over the laundry basket—the list goes on and on."

The word "weaker" is worth looking at in the Greek, because the Greek has many nuances that may not be apparent in the translation to English. The word is "asthenes," weaker in physical build (most men are larger with stronger bones and different muscle structure) and with some sickness (menstrual, pregnancy, childbirth, breastfeeding, even—we hate to admit—PMS). It also stems from the root word "stentho," which means more vulnerable in the spiritual realm.

Digging deeper to understand the roles of men and women, the Bible tells us what really happened in the Garden of Eden:

And it was not Adam who was deceived, but the woman being deceived, fell into transgression. (1 Timothy 2:14 NASB)

I am chagrined to admit I had thought I was wiser than my husband in a lot of ways (don't most wives?), and I surely didn't consider myself gullible. But the Bible was saying it was Eve, not Adam, who was deceived by the devil. And perhaps it is because of our softness, our femininity, our wanting to nurture and help the underdog that we are really more gullible than men. That isn't really a weakness, though, if you consider the goodness that underlies it. I mean, really, it looks like Adam didn't sin because he was deceived, he knew it was wrong and did it anyway. I think it also shows the power of a woman to convince a man of a thing, either good or bad.

Being more easily deceived may be the negative side of the female nature, but there is something wonderful about women: they are more trusting and open to ideas of others. Nearly all of the people asking for marriage counseling are women, because they are not afraid to ask for help and for others' opinion of their troubles. Men are built differently; they do not open up easily or ask for help. I remember tense times in the car when my husband would drive hours out of the way on a trip if he was unsure of direction rather than ask someone. Ever since they were stout little toddlers, men have said, "I can do it, watch me do it!"

Our present culture is in denial about a difference between men and women emotionally as well as physically. While it may seem a bit demeaning to say women are not as strong as men, it is a fact that, except for the unusual woman, women are smaller and their muscles can't be developed the same way as a man's. Female weight lifters generally have to take male hormones to accomplish the type of muscle bulk as a man. I don't know about you, but I like to see those muscles on a man, but there's something a little gross about a female with biceps the size of a ham. A woman could be more emotionally influenced than a man, making it a form of weakness if she changes a fair decision because of pity. Most experts agree that children raised by two parents, male and female, have a better chance of receiving balanced discipline and training because of the complementary approach of the parents.

Back to my life as a developing color consultant: studying clothing styles, I found that the uniqueness of each woman was shown off best by certain fabrics and prints. Even different fabrics and colors seemed to suit each sex. Since I had always been a sort of skinny, flat-chested girl with definitely not a mane of hair, I pounced on the idea that at least I could enhance femininity with colors and fabrics that boys generally avoided. Although one of my best colors happens to be brown, and my whole wardrobe was centered around shades of brown, I decided that I would look at my color palette and find more feminine colors. When I added peach, apricot, periwinkle blue, yellow greens, goldenrod—oh, the change it made! I felt like something came alive in me just by embracing the variety of colors God "embroidered" into my DNA. I also tried to add feminine soft, flowy fabrics. If we dress like a handyman, we shouldn't be surprised if our menfolk treat us like one. No, we want to be treated like a woman, even if we work hard. I know farm women who really do have to work hard outside, and naturally they have to wear sturdy clothing, but I have told them to at least wear your sweetest colors! Actually, by dressing like girls, we can help men and boys to do what they are asked to do in the scripture:

> In the same way, you husbands, live with your wives in an understanding way [with great gentleness and tact, and with an intelligent regard for the marriage relationship], as with someone physically weaker, since she is a woman. (1 Peter 3:7 AMP)

Don't let him forget it! My sister-in-law is amazing: she is a rancher's wife who can bush-hog, grade the driveway, lay up the stone on her house, ride the 4-wheeler to check on the cattle, just to name a few things. She and my brother built a beautiful home together, and she was right there on ladders helping to swing the huge logs into place, hanging dangerously out over space. She was grubby and dirty and sweaty a lot of the time, but somehow she was always *girl*. The jeans and shirts she wears are not ones a guy would pick. She has destroyed three hats as they flew off and got under the tractor, so she needs a new one, but maybe she will get a pink cowboy hat next time. She seems to know the difference between *helping hard* and *being hard*.

I think, though, that the real reason she seems feminine amidst all her hard work is *attitude*. She looks at all her husband has to do running his ranch and business, with the incredible amount of extra work during the 4 years it took to build their house, and she tries to see ways that she can *help*. She says, "I can't do wiring or plumbing, but I can learn to drive a tractor! Also, I don't build fences, but I can clean out the barn for him. He would never ask, because it is a dirty job, but for love of him, I do it." Anything that is in her realm of possibility she is willing to do to be kind and gentle and helpful. No wonder my brother thinks she is a wonder, a heavenly woman.

An update on this heavenly sister-in-law: she told me this very morning, as I was writing, "I just came in from a task and I had to laugh. It was exactly what we have been talking about in our heavenly woman study. Charley has been fussing about an area of his work truck for months. Maybe a year. It is the side tool area with a pull down door. It was a shambles. Last night I asked if I could help him. He said he would love 15 minutes of my time just to pull everything out. He was overwhelmed just looking at it. I pulled it all out, put it in "like" piles, and vacuumed it. He is out there now putting it back in—and he is thrilled! He said he couldn't thank me enough. It was so easy for me! It took so little time and effort. But it was a HUGE help to him. He could have done it himself—but he said it would have taken him twice as long. I was able to do something for him that was easy and fun for me and a headache and stress for him. I'll bet he hangs the towel rods today that I have been wanting for weeks!"

God had that attitude in mind when he saw that Adam needed someone to come alongside him and be his "help-meet." God put Adam in the garden first, but saw that "It is not good for man to be alone." God designed all the animals and brought them before Adam, but although some were helpful to him, none was a companion, so God designed Eve. When Adam saw Eve, the Bible says he said, "Pa ha maw!!!" The Hebrew literally means "This is *it*! She is part of me!" The heavenly woman learns what parts of her husband need help and is willing to help fill in that gap.

> Now the LORD God said, "It is not good (beneficial) for the man to be alone; I will make him a helper [one who balances him—a counterpart who is] suitable and complementary for him." (Genesis 2:18 AMP)

> Your adornment must not be merely external— braiding the hair, and wearing gold jewelry, or putting on dresses; 4 but let it be the hidden person of the heart, with the imperishable quality of a gentle and quiet spirit, which is precious in the sight of God. (1 Peter 3:3,4 NASB)

Trying to wear more feminine clothing is just "icing on the cake," not our true feminine beauty, which is "the hidden person of the heart, with the imperishable quality of a gentle and quiet spirit" (verse 4). As I read this verse, what jumped out at me was the word "gentle." The vision of a woman who could do all the things a woman does, and have the power she has over her children, her home, and even over her husband, yet remains gentle, is a very beautiful thought. In the rear view mirror of my mind, I could see myself yelling at small children who annoyed me, and I winced as I saw my attitude toward a husband who I thought wasn't doing things the way I thought he should. Oh, those immature expectations. It was water under the bridge concerning a husband now—but I was intrigued to learn ways to show gentleness along with the firmness needed to guide my children. More to come on that later!

Peter actually starts Chapter 3 with a serious admonition about the woman's inner goodness and reverent behavior, before he continues the above verses about external adornment. I could see a plan emerging that differed from the one I had used in my marriage:

> In the same way, you wives, be submissive to your own husbands so that even if any *of* them are disobedient to the word, they may be won without a word by the behavior of their wives, as they observe your chaste and respectful behavior. Your adornment must not be merely external—braiding the hair, and wearing gold jewelry, or putting on dresses; but let it be the hidden person of the heart, with the imperishable quality of a gentle and quiet spirit, which is precious in the sight of God. For in this way in former times the holy women also, who hoped in God, used to adorn themselves, being submissive to their own husbands; [6] just as Sarah obeyed Abraham, calling him lord, and you have become her children if you do what is right without being frightened by any fear. (1 Peter 3:1-5)

I was starting to see just how much I had to learn, and some of the verses were hard to understand, especially in our modern culture. I read in Ephesians that it is a great mystery; but it was one that I wanted to get to the bottom of.

> And the two shall become one flesh. This mystery is great; but I am speaking with reference to Christ and the church. Nevertheless, each individual among you also is to love his own wife even as himself, and the wife must see to it that she respects her husband. (Ephesians 5:31—33, NASB)

Best-selling author Larry Christensen, in *The Christian Family*, outlines how serious our attitudes are in marriage, since we are to show the world a picture of the relationship of Christ and His Church:

> The highest love of God to man was shown in the sacrifice of Christ...Between the Church and Christ there exists a bond of love more holy, tender and firm than any which ever existed between God and man. In Christianity, there is set before man and wife the task of representing on earth this union between Christ and His Church—an image of self-sacrifice, devotion, and fidelity....

He says that the Christian family doesn't exist for its own benefit, but to bring glory and honor to God. I had never liked the idea of "submission" to a husband, but this was shedding new light on it. I imagined that it would take a heavenly woman to accept a holy role of submission to a husband the same holy way Jesus submitted to God the Father!

I saw that although wives and husbands are equal in worth, our roles are different, and we are gifted with the qualities needed for each of our roles. I know from my own sorry experience, and also from watching the world go by, that it doesn't work very well for women to boss their husbands, or try to tell them what to do. Is it worth demanding your own way if strife results and love dies a little? Most of our marriages start out with us being so much one flesh that we want to share everything—all our time and activities—but that can be killed off if we don't nurture the relationship by fulfilling our role that we are made for. If we are soft and feminine to *win* the man in the first place, how did we think we could *keep* him if we get bossy and hard to please? Our role as the feminine part of the couple includes all sorts of feminine mystique and intuition, and if we are smart, we can win a battle without a firing shot. I like the scene in the movie *My Big Fat Greek Wedding* where the mother tells the grown daughter, "The man may be the head of the house, but the woman is the neck, and we can turn the head any way we want." That is not to say that we are to manipulate the husband or undermine his direction, but we can have valid input and insight, and we have the feminine tools to be a good influence.

You would think that women would naturally love their husbands; but God knows that even though we start out that way, our natures are such that we want to manage things and not be told what to do. After a while, we get annoyed with the way our husbands don't fall into line with what we want, suggest, or even demand. We say we "fall out of love," but actually we stop being loving. That is a downward spiral for a marriage, but it doesn't have to happen that way.

Once we start asking God for *His* plan for our lives, or to fix our marriage if that is our situation, we find an astonishing thing: that the Scriptures tell the older women to take time to encourage the younger women to "love their husbands,...to be kind." At first I disagreed with God; *I loved my husband, he just quit loving me back*. Whoa, not so fast. God knows that after the excitement of the courtship and the romance of the wedding, the real everyday life may kill our emotions of love for the man. He knows we have to learn how to love with God's kind of love. It begins with obedience to God, of course, where we say "no" to our old life and "yes" to God. Then it filters down to obedience to authorities and even respect for our ex-suitor turned caveman; now God instructs us to love this man who no longer courts us, who has a lot of faults that weren't evident in courtship. This time, God wants us to love in a new way, a gentle and kind way, where we adapt to our husband, looking for ways to be a complement to him.

> Older women similarly are to be...teaching what is right and good, so that they may encourage the young women to tenderly love their husbands and their children, to be sensible, pure, makers of a home [where God is honored], good-natured, being subject to their own husbands. (Titus 2:4,5 AMP).

> We have come to know and have believed the love which God has for us. God is love, and the one who abides in love abides in God, and God abides in him. By this, love is perfected with us.... (1 John 4:16,17 NCB)

It can seem hard to actually live out God's plan for a truly feminine Christian woman. It may seem that God is asking us to give up *our* way and fit into another person's plan, and that goes against all the world has taught us about being our own person and not being submissive to anyone. But now, too late for my marriage, I could see that God loves us with an unconditional love, and will give us the kind of love that can transform our hearts from hard and rebellious and antagonistic hearts to soft and gentle and loving and helpful hearts. Heavenly woman hearts.

My thoughts drift again to the beginning—*literally* the beginning—in the Garden of Eden. God had made man with grand design for him to rule over the world God had made. However, he realized that the garden was lonely; the nights were even lonelier and long for the man, so God took pity on him and gave him a woman, "a helper suitable for him." The Hebrew word for helper is "ezer," which literally means to "surround, protect, and help." Does it surprise you to learn that our feminine role, while being the "weaker" one, includes the idea of protecting him and surrounding him and helping him? It did surprise me! Men do seem to be a little lost, generally, without a woman to help. That should convince us how important our "helping" role is. No wonder my sister-in-law has such a great love relationship with her husband, since she is constantly on the lookout for ways to help. I want to become a *hunter of ways to help.* It doesn't have to be helping a husband if he is already gone, but how about anyone in our sphere? What a delightful thought. A secret, happy, delighted helper! I want to learn that!

LIVING IT:

Be a hunter of ways to be a helper! I chuckle to think of the picture of Santa's happy little secret behind-the-scenes helpers. What if we can be God's feminine, gentle, happy secret helpers?

Practice being soft and gentle and adaptable instead of being demanding or bossy with those around us. If a husband suggests doing something that he would like to do but usually you don't, try saying, "Yes, let's do that!" instead of "But I want to do...."

Protect your mate, your kids, others by helping in their area of weakness: helping, not judging. If you help where they are weak, you will go up in the heavenly woman scale in their eyes. For instance, if your mate is messy in an area that he just can't seem to keep on top of, maybe quietly helping him, surprising him, will delight him. That protects him from others' bad opinion of him. Same with co-workers, children, parents. Don't speak of their weakness to others, but help cover them up by your love.

Also try wearing something more feminine in fabric, color, and style to reinforce the soft and gentle image. We can be a strong person while being gentle and kind and feminine. Remember, we are the one to "surround, protect and help" those we love.

FOR FUN:

Think about fabrics that you wear. What clothing do you actually have in your closet that you love and get compliments in, and what fabric are they made of?

Think of different fabrics and details and decide which look more feminine, which are masculine: (put an M or F by each)

Chiffon_____ Tweed_____ Corduroy_____
Cashmere_____ Angora_____ Heavy wool_____
Leather_____ Duck_____ Canvas_____
Ruffles_____ Ribbons_____ Straight lines_____
Gathers_____
Maybe you can think of more: _____
Give away things that don't remind people around you that you are a girl!

Chapter 5

THE BELOVED WOMAN: BUILDING A HOUSE OF LOVE

> So, chosen by God for this new life of love, dress in the wardrobe God picked out for you: compassion, kindness, humility, quiet strength, discipline. Be even-tempered, content with second place, quick to forgive an offense. Forgive as quickly and completely as the Master forgave you. And regardless of what else you put on, wear love. It's your basic, all-purpose garment. Never be without it. (Colossians 3:12 – 14 MSG)

I had been working on starting up my color analysis business while working on trying to find my new normal as a single mom. The children were confused about why their dad was suddenly gone, and I couldn't explain it. The two littlest boys started wetting the bed again after being nice and dry, and I suspected it was the emotions of it all, but I didn't know how to fix it. My little girl was about eight, and was heartbroken. Freddy had always called her his little princess and had made a special fuss over her, but then dropped out of her daily life; she did a lot of crying at bedtime. How do you fix things for little ones?

Life was weird, and every way I turned, I couldn't seem to

fit in. The couples we had done things with didn't know how to relate to half of a couple, and I wasn't invited anymore. Even some religious family members added to my sadness by saying that they believed that a divorced woman can never remarry. I didn't know what to do with my life except try to get through each day, and I didn't even want to think about what the long, bleak future held. The church pastor told me that, frankly, it wasn't probable that I would ever remarry, because most men wouldn't want to take on four little kids and someone with a failed marriage. He of course didn't say it, but I wondered if he thought I wasn't all that great looking either. The old insecurities were still trying to add to my burden.

One day late in the summer, I was sitting on the top of the grassy hill that overlooked my house, watching the children play on the swing set, and reached down absentmindedly and plucked a clover blossom. I looked at it and was astonished to find it dry and brown. I expected it to be soft and pink, as it is in the summer. I suddenly realized that the summer was gone, that autumn was almost here. Then something really strange happened: it was what I suppose would be called a "vision." In my mind I saw a picture of a calendar, and the page was open to the month Freddy had finally left—just stuck there. I saw the pages turn slowly, one by one, until *August.* I think it was God letting me know that my life had been stuck, waiting for the marriage to resume, because that is all I had known. He showed me that it would never happen, and that I must get on with my life. He let me know that the chapters in my life were going to change soon, and *I was not to look back, but to just trust Him.* Amazed, I got to my feet and went down the hill to the house with new energy. *Life was not over; God was in control.*

Part of what God was showing me was that I needed to get out of our old fellowship group that Freddy and I had shared, and go to a "regular" Christian church. The pastor in our old fellowship pretty much wrote me off when I quit cleaning his house, and he "reassigned" me from being part of the close-knit group of leadership couples that met in his home group to a "lesser" group, unfamiliar to me. So not only was I rejected by my ex, but now tossed out of my home fellowship group. *Time to move on*, and I felt God was doing the leading. I took the children to a community church in the nearby village on a Sunday in late August. It was a nice little church, and the pastor was English, unusual for a rural church.

The very next day, he came to make a pastoral call, as was the custom in the rural churches in our area. Anyway, when the doorbell rang, and I opened the door and saw the young Englishman standing there, my heart really started acting up! It sounds strange, but it seemed to be thumping in my chest! I was shocked. I didn't know this pastor at all, so what was going on? I managed a polite visit, barely able to speak coherently. After he left, I went to my room and cried out to God. I said, basically, "God, what just happened there? I really don't need a man in my life. You know what terrible pain I have been through for years because of loving a man. *However,* if you are in this, and want me to not be afraid of it, then show me a sign. Let him show up at the concert I am taking the children to tomorrow night, and let him sit with me." (I didn't know that a lot of religious people say we shouldn't ask for a sign, but God evidently has patience with young Christians!)

As sure as I am sitting here writing this to you, this is what happened. The next evening, as the concert was just about to start, here came that English preacher, walking up the aisle. He saw me and seemed surprised. He asked if the seat next to me was taken, and, of course, it wasn't. God had saved it for him. I could hardly breathe all evening, wondering what God was doing.

We didn't date, but he found reasons to "swing by" to check on us quite often after that. With autumn coming on, nights could get quite frosty in our area in early September. Due to the oil crisis back then and skyrocketing fuel prices, most of us in my neighborhood had put in wood-burning stoves. One cold evening I was trying to get our too-green wood to burn, and he happened by. He chopped some wood and started the fire. We joked over the following years that he came and "lit my fire." Actually, we both felt from that first concert event that God was bringing us together, and we separately prayed a lot for guidance. What did *God* want? *I* had chosen a husband before, and it was all wrong. This time, I wanted only God's choice.

My birthday was in November, and he gave me a beautiful card, signed, "Will you marry me? --Thomas." I knew it was God's will to accept. I didn't know what it would mean as far as where we would live or what we would live on. His church position had been just an interim appointment, and he was between churches, so he was doing odd jobs. That we were practically penniless didn't seem to even occur to us. God had a plan, and that was enough.

Thomas and I were married in January, and it sure has been an adventure. What started out as just God's idea bloomed into a beautiful and wonderful love between us. The basis of our relationship was Jesus Christ, so as we each tried to follow Him closely, we would find ourselves on the same path, going in the same direction. I'm sure, now, that is why the Bible tells us not to be unequally yoked with an unbeliever—for what fellowship does God have with the devil? And fellowship is what our women's hearts crave. Men's hearts do too, but often they don't know it until we, with the wonderful unique woman gifts and ways that God has given us, lead them into a love partnership they bask in. A man of God who is loved by a Spirit-filled Christian woman who is trying to fit in with God's plan will find himself so deeply in love that he can hardly believe it. He, then, in turn, adores her and gives her the love and gentleness and care that she has deeply wanted all her life.

> Do not be bound together with unbelievers; for what partnership have righteousness and lawlessness, or what fellowship has light with darkness? (2 Corinthians 6:14 NASB)

What do women want more than anything? To be loved. That's *beloved*. We do all sorts of things to be loved, or to try to be loved. The obvious surface things we do to get "loved" in the first place—as a teenager—are surface: makeup, hair, clothes. The Bible indicates that real love will come from inner beauty, but it is a rare teen who thinks, "I want to be beautiful on the inside." And we *do* need to make sure our hair, makeup and clothing are as attractive as possible (*attractive* means to attract, to bring to one, or to try to get loved). Indeed, young (even older) men are usually *attracted* to us because of our looks at first. Maybe that's God's plan—but I do know that all that quickly sours if the inside isn't beautiful. The man may withdraw his attention from a woman who "trapped" him with her beauty but becomes a burden of high maintenance, always wanting more attention. Of course, what she is really wanting is to feel *beloved*. That is what he wants to feel too, but he is sort of unconscious about how to get there. We have to help him. And the Bible tells us how! There *is* a Bible way for women to live that will make them become beloved by all those who know them, whether husband, child, parent, or associate.

Love cannot be demanded. It comes naturally (or should I say supernaturally?) as we offer our hard hearts to God and ask Him to beautify them. I found it helpful to read the Message version of 1 Peter 3:4,5, which adds a contemporary understanding to the more traditional versions. It shows us what pleases God, as well as our husband and our families:

> The same goes for you wives: Be good wives to your husbands, responsive to their needs. There are husbands who, indifferent as they are to any

words about God, will be captivated by your life of holy beauty. What matters is not your outer appearance—the styling of your hair, the jewelry you wear, the cut of your clothes—but your inner disposition.

Cultivate inner beauty, the gentle, gracious kind that God delights in. The holy women of old were beautiful before God that way, and were good, loyal wives to their husbands. Sarah, for instance, taking care of Abraham, would address him as "my dear husband." You'll be true daughters of Sarah if you do the same, unanxious and unintimidated. (1 Peter 3:1 – 6 MSG)

The Hebrew word for beloved is *dowd*. It means literally a boiling pot, and figuratively means a deep stirring of emotion of love. It also can mean "uncle," with connotations of friendly, familiar, trusted person yet one who stirs great feelings of respect and love. Woman is gifted with what she needs to stir these up!

The wise woman builds her house, But the foolish tears it down with her own hands. (Proverbs 14:1, NASB)

A woman's house is her nest. When she builds her house, she is not using brick and mortar. She is stirring emotions of love and building bonds that grow strong to help love to last a lifetime. One day I was trying to put up drapery rods in my sun room, usually not a difficult job. But the wood was very hard, and as I got the screws about three-fourths of the way in, they stubbornly refused to finish going in. Perhaps it was the angle I was holding the screw gun, up on a ladder, or maybe that I couldn't get enough weight behind it, but I finally stopped. I thought I might strip the screws, and I wished my hubby was home with his extra strength. When he came home, he was able to finish the job in a minute (without breaking a fingernail).

I thought of a sort of modern day parable that fits into the above Proverbs 14:1 idea:

A certain woman wanted a shelf hung in her home, and she asked her husband to hang it for her. He just didn't get around to it, and she mentioned it, but it was never a good time, as he really was busy. Finally, one day she hung it herself, but she left the screws out a little bit. She was actually having trouble getting the screws all the way in. When her husband saw it, she said, "Honey, I know you planned to hang it, but I know with that extra job you took on and everything, you just didn't have time, so I tried to do it. It is ok, but those screws got really hard to finish getting all the way in. I think since you are stronger, you can get them flush in." And he did. Another woman asked her husband to put up a shelf, and he agreed but also didn't get around to it. She mentioned it several times, gave hints about it, then finally just hung it herself. The screws were hard to get in all the way, but, a bit angry and determined, she kept after it until finally the screws were in. She did it. She found that she could do it just fine without him and told him so when he got home. The first woman was not being manipulative; she was being smart, in not only getting her shelf hung, but in "building her house." The second woman got the shelf hung, but was she using her feminine wisdom to "build her house" or to "tear it down with her own hands"? Our house is so much more than the property we live in. For us women, it is where we want to be loved, and our mate wants to be loved. Nurturing is more important than shelving.

One of the things Thomas did when we were first married was to read the Song of Solomon to me as part of our Bible reading. I had never considered the poetry of the Bible could be part of marriage! That Bible book will always bring special stirrings of love to me, especially these verses that talk about being the beloved (of God and man). It is poetry written as a duet, some verses by the bride and some by the bridegroom:

The bride:

> And you, my dear lover—you're so handsome!
> And the bed we share is like a forest glen.
> We enjoy a canopy of cedars
> enclosed by cypresses, fragrant and green ...
> My lover is mine, and I am his.
> Nightly he strolls in our garden,
> Delighting in the flowers
> until dawn breathes its light and night slips away.
> Turn to me, dear lover.
> Come like a gazelle.
> Leap like a wild stag
> on delectable mountains! (Song of Solomon 1:16,17 MSG)

> The groom:
> Get up, my dear bride,
> Fair and beautiful lover—come to me!
> Look around you: winter is over;... Spring flowers are in blossom all over.

> The bride:
> My dear lover glows with health—
> red-blooded, radiant!
> He's one in a million.
> There's no one quite like him! ...

> The groom:
> I'm spoiled for anyone else!
> Your beauty, within and without, is absolute,
> dear lover, close companion. (Song of Solomon 2:10—14 MSG)

Romantic love based on God as the glue that holds a couple together is an amazing love. I had never known a love like that!

Classic literature has lots of stories that illustrate beautiful love. I especially enjoy Charles Dickens' *David Copperfield.* (Not to be confused with the magician David Copperfield!) David's first wife, darling Dora, captivates his heart with her beauty and her enchanting charm. The bliss he envisioned when he courted her eluded him, as she was hopeless at managing household affairs, and would rather play with her little doggie than anything. She was like a pretty child, but not an intellectual partner. After she tragically passed away, he married Agnes, a more plain but honest and true friend he had loved all his life, and he found fulfillment in a comfortable and well-run home and deep companionship, as well as passion and resulting children. He did, however, in pensive moods, think how he missed the delightful little ways of Dora. I think it is a good word picture of how a man is happier if he could have Dora and Agnes rolled into one, and we would be smart heavenly women if we don't neglect either one.

Look at Abraham and Sarah, how he loved her greatly after she developed inner beauty as well as outer beauty. (The kings all raved over her beauty!) How he mourned for her when she passed away, even when he was 120 years old.

What then can we do to become beloved? Helen Andelin wrote rather strong words in her classic, *Fascinating Womanhood:*

> Love is not reserved for the young, the single, the beautiful. It is reserved for those who arouse it in a man [or son or daughter or parent, etc.]. If a man does not love with heart and soul, it is the woman's fault. *A man ceases to adore and cherish a woman after marriage because she ceases to do the things which arouse these feelings.* If she obeys the [biblical] laws upon which love is based, she can kindle a deep and stirring feeling within

his heart.... The art of becoming beloved is not a difficult accomplishment for woman, because it is based upon her natural [God-given] instincts. In our complicated, highly civilized life of today, many of her natural instincts have become dulled or suppressed. She needs but to re-discover that which belongs to her by nature.

(I need to say right here that I don't agree completely with Andelin when she says if a man does not love the wife, it is her fault—I think she has some insight on things we might have missed in our modern culture, but from my own experience, I respectfully say that when my first marriage broke up, I was at fault in some ways, but so was he!)

I have always remembered what Andelin wrote about the famous Taj Mahal, and I quote:

In the city of Agra in Northern India stands the Taj Mahal. Although it was built in the seventeenth century, it is still one of the most beautiful buildings in the world and the most costly in existence. It was built by the Indian ruler Shah Jahan, in memory of his favorite wife, Mumtaz-i-Mahal which means 'Bride of the Palace.' Mumtaz died at the birth of her fourteenth child. The Shah had other wives, but bestowed such honor to only one—Mumtaz. Where is OUR Taj Mahal? Have we earned such love and devotion from our man? Mumtaz was beloved. The love she earned from the Shah was a celestial type of love, love in its highest form. It lifts it out of the mediocre and places it in the heavens where love belongs. It is flowers rather than weeds—the banquet rather than the crumbs." (Author's note: I don't imply from this that polygamy is God's will!)

My new marriage was based on God's choice of mate to start with, and then continued by both of us following God together. I was enjoying a banquet with the humble English preacher, after years of crumbs. And it all came from starting to look to God for answers!

LIVING IT:

If you are married, ask God to show you ways to arouse emotional love from your mate. We have talked before about being more feminine, which is one way. Another is to be pleasant on the eyes. Another is to find ways to let your man protect and help you when you need him. In your notebook, start a new page to list any ideas you have about ways to draw forth divine love from your mate. You will actually be doing him a great service!

Those of you who are not married, think about other relationships that are not romantic, but still are often described as "beloved:" "beloved mother," "beloved daughter," etc. Think of ways we can become beloved people. What can we do? Be?

FOR FUN:

Watch *David Copperfield* by Charles Dickens if you can. I like the Masterpiece Theater version with Daniel Radcliffe. Look for what attributes each wife, Dora and Agnes, have that earned love and devotion from David.

Chapter 6

THE FORGIVING WOMAN —
A 490-WEEK PROJECT

One of the delights of my soul that first winter of being married to my preacher husband was having a soul mate who loved God's Word as much as I did. More, really. He was up before the birds every morning, feasting on the Manna and seeking God.

It had started on the honeymoon, actually. He served me Communion our first evening, and we had prayer together, and I felt almost like we were being given a new start in life, an Adam and Eve, with the awesome new world before us.

> The Man said, "Finally! Bone of my bone, flesh of my flesh!" ...
> Therefore a man leaves his father and mother and embraces his wife. They become one flesh.
> (Genesis 2:23,24 MSG)

When I awoke the next morning, he was already dressed and sitting quietly in a chair reading his Bible. And that's how it has been for about 40 years! Oh, over time I found that my Man of God was human and not perfect, just as he found out that I was very human—but one thing I could always count on was that he would be living and learning God's ways as he continually read his Bible. That's a foundation that will never crumble or give way, and from the first has brought a feeling of security to my scattered soul. Whatever shadows fell across our path, I could count on him falling back on the Word of God to shine light on the way and give us answers.

> When two of you get together on anything at all on earth and make a prayer of it, my Father in heaven goes into action. And when two or three of you are together because of me, you can be sure that I'll be there. (Matthew 18:20 MSG)

One of the first shadows that cast darkness across the blindingly beautiful new life together was one I least expected, but should have. Blind I was. Thomas and I were barely back from our honeymoon when Freddy, who had said he just wanted "out" and didn't want children or family, declared he would have his children every other weekend. Now, from the perspective of maturity and older age, that sounds very reasonable and expected. Also, from a more healed frame of mind, I now wish I had just been glad that Freddy wanted to show love to his kids, so they didn't have to feel deserted. Why I didn't expect it, I don't know, but there it was, and I felt so bitter and angry to have to send my little ones off with him, to spend weekends with him and his new wife. The kids came back full of sugar, and my insides *writhed*. The two littlest boys were hyperactive and were different boys on sugar; it took three days to get them back to their normal selves. I had to fumigate their clothing as soon as they arrived and wash them down to get cigarette smell out of their hair. (I'm sure Freddy didn't smoke, but perhaps it came from bowling alleys, as Freddy was an avid bowler?) Whatever, I let the weeds of bitterness grow in my garden.

Wasn't it bad enough that he didn't want us and rejected us (as I interpreted his wanting out)? But now when I finally was having the chance to make a pleasant life for the children and myself, he was back. Not *back* back, but back in my life. Back in their lives. I wish I could have considered it a good thing for the children, but blinded by rejection, I didn't.

That was a reality that somehow completely caught me off guard. Having had no experience with divorce (mine was the first in our whole extended family), I didn't know that it *never goes away*. I suppose I thought that since the old marriage was dead and gone, I could be done with it and have an all-new life. Well, I had a new life, for sure: one where I would have to learn to use the past to learn new ways of living and forgiving.

In the early years, I blamed Freddy for the whole affair. Literally. And every other Friday I *writhed* all over again as I packed the little overnight bags. It wasn't very long until my "resident minister" helped me to see that I was needing to deal with forgiveness so that I could have peace. I did pray, "Lord, help me to forgive him." And I would feel better. Yay, I had forgiven him, and all was good. Until the next Friday. The feeling was back. So I would go again to God and deal with forgiveness. "God, I thought I had forgiven him, but I feel it all over again. How long does this go on?" St. Peter was troubled the same way, and finally voiced his question to Jesus:

> At that point Peter got up the nerve to ask, "Master, how many times do I forgive a brother or sister who hurts me? Seven?"
>
> Jesus replied, "Seven! Hardly. Try seventy times seven." (Matthew 18:21,22 MSG)

Four hundred and ninety times. Wow! I saw what Jesus was saying: not that a person had done four hundred and ninety mean things that I had to forgive, but that it isn't a "once and done" thing. Every other Friday I would get the opportunity to re-energize the forgiveness that I had decided on in obedience to God's Word, even if it would be four hundred and ninety Fridays. That would probably be the entire child visitation years! I wondered if God was thinking about the forgiveness required after divorce when he said "seventy times seven"!

As I read what the Bible said about forgiveness, I realized that I had *no choice* but to forgive, since I had received such wonderful forgiveness from God for all my own failures. Jesus put it so well:

> For this reason, the kingdom of heaven is like a king who wanted to settle accounts with his slaves. As he began settling his accounts, a man who owed ten thousand talents was brought to him. Because he was not able to repay it, the lord ordered him to be sold, along with his wife, children, and whatever he possessed, and repayment to be made. Then the slave threw himself to the ground before him, saying, 'Be patient with me, and I will repay you everything.' The lord had compassion on that slave and released him, and forgave him the debt. After he went out, that same slave found one of his fellow slaves who owed him one hundred silver coins. So he grabbed him by the throat and started to choke him, saying, 'Pay back what you owe me!' Then his fellow slave threw himself down and begged him, 'Be patient with me, and I will repay you.' But he refused. Instead, he went and threw him in prison until he repaid the debt. When his fellow slaves saw what had happened, they were very upset and went and told their lord everything that had taken place. Then his lord called the first slave and said to him, 'Evil slave! I forgave you all that debt because you begged me! Should you not have shown mercy to your fellow slave, just as I showed it to you?' (Matthew 18:23—33 NEB)

So, God helped me to stop wrestling with whether or not I

had forgiven, and to just rest in the fact that I would get to re-energize forgiveness each time I was reminded of the hurt. I did have to just *accept*, eventually, that the reality of divorce is that the ex is going to be part of the scene. (The case should be made that the children *need* to feel loved by their biological father, to be healthy.) We have all heard the Serenity Prayer. I didn't know that there was more than the four familiar lines, but I found it one day and cut it out and put it on the fridge:

> God, grant me the serenity
> to accept the things I cannot change,
> the courage to change the things I can,
> and the wisdom to know the difference.
> Living one day at a time,
> enjoying one moment at a time;
> accepting hardship as a pathway to peace;
> taking, as Jesus did,
> this sinful world as it is,
> not as I would have it;
> trusting that You will make all things right
> if I surrender to Your will;
> so that I may be reasonably happy in this life
> and supremely happy with You forever in the next.
> Amen.
> --Reinhold Niebuhr

I needed to accept what I could not change. And more, "taking, as Jesus did, this sinful world as it is, not as I would have it; trusting that You will make all things right...."

The saddest part is that although, with God's wonderful help over time, it got easier for me, it got harder for the children. In the beginning when they were little, they were glad enough to get to see their dad again on their visitation weekends, and he was truly the "sugar daddy," as most exes are, cramming their weekends full of fun activities and fast food. However, that gradually abated, as he went through two more marriages and many miles between him and his kids. But fast forward to now, about 40 years later. Our children are middle-aged, and their father, who has been absent for most of their years and with whom they have little relationship, of course expects them to accommodate him and his current wife whenever he wants to come stay with them, because he does love them. But because of our choices, they hardly know him, and they don't know his wife. They feel guilty if they want to avoid hosting them because it is awkward, or if they "can't work it out." I am sobered by how my choices early in my adult life have affected my children *all* their lives. As a young mother, I thought that although divorce is awful, at least I would have him out of my life. What I didn't realize was he would always be in the children's lives, for better or worse. What serious vows we take when we marry and say "I do," for better or for worse; we just don't realize we are taking those vows for the children.

Now, so many years later, I don't blame Freddy like I did in the midst of the pain of rejection. He did wrong, for sure, but wasn't he as much a victim of Satan, who had blinded us both for so long from seeing the beauty of God's plan for our lives? Realizing this, I feel even more grateful to God, who has forgiven me so completely for the damage that I had a part in.

> And the Lord's servant must not engage in heated disputes but be kind toward all, an apt teacher, patient, correcting opponents with gentleness. Perhaps God will grant them repentance and then knowledge of the truth and they will come to their senses and escape the devil's trap where they are held captive to do his will. (2 Timothy 2:24—26 NET)

Forgiveness is beneficial to both the forgiven and the forgiver. Artist and poet Judith Cantrell wrote: "We don't forgive people because they deserve to be forgiven. We forgive them because we don't deserve to go on hurting for something someone else did." Think about unforgiveness as a heavy burden that we can continue to drag all through our days, or we can forgive, and leave it behind, free to become a kinder, gentler heavenly woman, full of grace. Grace, is of course, "unmerited favor," so we give favor to one who doesn't deserve it. That's pure forgiveness. And we can pray for others to forgive us in the same way.

Forgiveness was the first big lesson I learned in my new marriage, perhaps because that was so necessary for us as a new couple to go forward in ministry. Forgiveness sets us free, and it actually sets free those whom we forgive. When I accepted reality and learned to better live out forgiveness, our marriage and my life took on a new dimension. Although I still stumble at it at times, basically I tend now to overlook wrongs and forgive, because I also have been forgiven. That's big.

Jump ahead to forty years later; God did an amazing miracle. The forgiveness thing was something I had to work hard at concerning Freddy, for many years, and there was always a lingering feeling of bitterness in my heart that I had to push away. But God is so patient! One day as I was in church this past spring, I felt the Holy Spirit speak to me. I felt Him say, "It is time to finally finish your forgiveness with Freddy, and clear things up." I was scared, and wanted to run and hide, rather than contact Freddy. I had not seen him or talked to him for many years. I had x'd my ex out of my life. Still, the words from God followed me home from church, and didn't leave me. I asked my grown kids if I should contact him, or just let sleeping dogs lie. I was thinking (hoping) they would say to let it be. But they were pleasantly surprised, and said that I should absolutely do it. I texted him and asked if it was ok to talk. He phoned me, and I was astonished at the miracle that happened. It was as if every shred of bitterness and anger dissipated like fog in the sunshine, and we had a very good conversation. We agreed that the kids are both of ours, and that as adults we should be able to pick up the phone to tell one another about events in the kids' lives. When I shared it with the kids later, I could see that a huge load went off their shoulders! I hadn't realized how hard they had tried all those years to "manage" us. I praise God for His wonderful work!

LIVING IT

Are there big (or little) hurts in your life that you have not forgiven? Or perhaps you have forgiven but need to re-energize the forgiveness every time you think of it? If you have been forgiven, why not offer that same grace to any who have hurt you? Doing so will release the power of God to change some things—try it and see the wonders of God, who understands your pain, and has a plan to redeem the situation and give you joy.

FOR FUN

Make your own bookmark! Now that you know more than most people about the Serenity Prayer, why not make a bookmark reminder for yourself of how this isn't a perfect world, that we want to accept the sinful world as it is, not the way we would have it, and surrender it to God. You can make it anyway you like, depending on how artsy or crafty you are. If you are a zero in the art department, you can always cut out a pretty flower from a catalog, and print or type words. Maybe you can practice script writing, practice a little colored pencil or watercolor. Maybe stitch something. Put your bookmark in your Bible or your journal—where it can remind you that no matter how sinful the world around you is, you can surrender it to God and have serenity.

Chapter 7

THE HOLY WOMAN— BEING RESPECTFUL

My own Reverend never ceased to amaze me, as I experienced what it was like to be married to a "Man of God," as one of my sons referred to him in the beginning of our courtship. The first and most obvious thing was that when I awoke in the morning, he was always already up and dressed and reading the Bible, seeking direction from the Lord. Direction was important at that time in our lives, because he knew that he had received "the call" to full-time ministry, but he was not currently in a church pulpit.

Back in England, when he was a very young man, he had been praying in his bedroom and heard God speak to him that he was to be a minister and go to Bible School. Nobody in his "working class" family had ever gone to college—*unheard of!* (England still has classes of society, with noticeable divides between servant class, working class, professionals, gentility and royalty.) He was a quiet, introverted young man who had not done any public speaking, and even his local church pastor discouraged his wanting to study for ministry because of his shyness. But, he was certain he had heard God, and pressed on, finding a way to go to a Bible college at Surrey, south of London. Then he was assigned to small churches around the Midlands of England, until one day he heard from God again, this time to "go to America." Again, nobody in their strata of society had ever done this, but he determined he would go. When he had saved enough for a plane ticket, he came to the good old USA with $5 in his pocket, just like a movie script. He was given a church position in Wisconsin. From then on he had been in ministry in several states, first with independent churches, then with the Methodists, and then the independent church in our village. Until now.

He knew God would show him the next step, so he did a lot of asking and seeking. The promise is that if we really seek, we will find. The Greek word for "seek" literally means to "beat a path," so I think it means keep going over the same ground, asking and looking for God's path, until you find it. Here, the use of Greek present imperative (asking, seeking, knocking; Matthew 7:7, 8) emphasizes persistent, constant prayer. In grammar class, we all learned that "imperative mood" is used when something absolutely has to be done and cannot be put off. Imperative is from Latin *imperare,* "to command," and its original use was for a verb form expressing a command: *Do it!*

> Ask, and it shall be given you; seek, and ye shall find; knock, and it shall be opened unto you. (Matthew 7:7 KJV)

> And ye shall seek me, and find me, when ye shall search for me with all your heart.
> (Jeremiah 29:13 KJV)

> When you come looking for me, you'll find me. Yes, when you get serious about finding me and want it more than anything else, I'll make sure you won't be disappointed. (Jeremiah 29:13 MSG)

The Hebrew word used for "looking for me" in the Jeremiah quote above is *baqash–* to seek, search, or consult. This word has been used to describe seeking something that's lost or missing, to seek one's face, or to aim at, devote oneself to, and be concerned about something.

The house I was awarded in the divorce was large, with a huge mortgage payment; Thomas did spend time "beating a path" to God's door for an answer to our future. He had had no trouble getting a job planting seedlings for a nursery, since in England he had done a lot of greenhouse work while in Bible college, but the paycheck was small. It was just something to bring a little income in while he was seeking God's ministry place for him. I was content to have our special relationship and to have some stability for the children, and although I understood the serious quest he was on to be back in a pulpit, each day's joy was enough for me. I was sure God would give us what we needed.

I had no experience in managing money, which was soon to become apparent. The very first week of our marriage I went to meet Thomas at his nursery job at lunchtime on payday, and I went to cash his check, then went to get groceries. It wasn't a large check like I was used to in my first marriage, but it bought the groceries. I think it was a shock to Thomas when he found I spent it all, but he never said anything. He just beat a path to God all the more.

One morning when I got up and went downstairs, Thomas said he had been up praying during the night, and God had spoken to him these words: "When were you last on track?" As he had pondered those words, he realized that the answer was when he was a minister with the Methodist church, several years before. When he told me that, it just seemed "right," somehow, and we agreed that he would contact the District Superintendent of the district that he had been associated with. He made an appointment, and made the hour and a half trip.

The Superintendent gave him a very chilly, perhaps hostile, reception. That Thomas had been a Methodist minister and then left to pastor other churches was not exactly in his favor, and it looked like the interview was going nowhere. Thomas sent a silent prayer up for God's help, and later told me that it was amazing—immediately as the prayer went up, there came a change over the Superintendent and he warmed up and said he thought he could find a church for him in the next round of ministerial assignments.

In the meantime, Thomas said he felt that God was also directing him to complete his schooling. The Bible college in England didn't have equivalent here, and he said he thought he should go back to the university where he had taken classes when he was a Methodist student pastor several years back. That meant selling the house and moving to the college town in the next county. I didn't mind at all, because I had the sense that we were on a grand adventure! I had no fear of the unknown, because I felt certain that God was in charge.

We listed the house with a real estate agent, who said it was a slow market, and it might take a bit of time. However, it was incredible: the house sold immediately. We packed what we thought we would need, and there were piles and heaps of things from the first marriage that we gave away. We went to the college town, found a little rental house right near campus, and we moved. What a whirlwind. And what a move! It was -20 degrees Fahrenheit and the snow was 2 feet deep. Even the moving van battery wouldn't turn over. Too cold! I had wanted to lift some roses to take with us, but without dynamite, there was not going to be any digging in the frozen garden! Where we lived the soil often froze a foot or more deep. I didn't know it then, but my love of flowers was going to take a different turn. A lifetime of living in parsonages and moving every few years would teach me the simple joys of annual flowers, not the long-lived roses and perennials I had loved. An older wiser woman once said that a Christian wife should make all her dreams portable. Probably she was talking about a minister's wife!

Thomas enrolled in college, and spring came. The Methodist

assignments are made during the spring, as the various district superintendents meet in hallowed halls and shuffle their pastors like cards until all the vacancies are filled. We didn't hear anything, and summer was coming on. One day we were sitting at the kitchen table looking at a map of our state, asking God to show us where we should go. Then the phone rang, and it was a superintendent offering Thomas a church in a rural town right where he had been looking at on the map when the phone call came! Having God be the director of our lives was a whole new experience for me. But I really had no idea yet what that would mean for me.

We moved into the church's parsonage, which was a pleasant home in a peaceful and pretty village in the hills outside of a city. In that part of the country, parsonages are provided empty, so we moved in all our own furniture and appliances and it was instantly home. I loved it. It had several acres, so the children had room to run and play, and I had space to have a large vegetable garden. The church building was within an easy walk. The people were friendly and happy to have a "young family with children."

I looked forward to being part of a women's Bible study group, remembering the close ties I had had with other women in my earlier years. We had sat in each other's kitchens and traded our amazing Christian-woman books and stories and babysat each other's kids. But it was a shock to me to find that I was no longer one of the women: I was "the minister's wife." Sounds like a movie title—but I had no script. What was expected of me? The women were uncomfortable having me to their homes, wanting to have them all cleaned and ready for a visit by "the minister's wife." And who did they expect to lead any Bible study? MOI! ME!

Thankfully I don't sing or play the piano, so at least those jobs went to someone else. But leading Bible School, organizing the nursery, teaching Sunday School, heading up the women's groups, and being present at every event fell to me. It was just expected. That was what traditional ministers' wives did. And they were also expected to speak kindly and be proper in dress and protocol. Their homes were to be immaculate and their children well mannered. They were on a pedestal. Wow, I had a steep learning curve!

Some wives that I met through district functions deeply resented the traditional role, but I found I really liked it. I'm a romantic traditionalist at heart anyway, and I felt like I was playing a part in an old-time play, a time before the women's revolution of the 60's and 70's. Our little village was still running the way it had forever. The little post office was held open a few hours a day by one of the housewives. The grocery store had a pop cooler on the porch and oiled floors. Everyone was related, it seemed, and church was like a family affair. They adored their little English minister, and his "lovely family."

So, married to a "man of God," I fell into the role of a "holy woman." The outer role was a pleasant one, but at home in the parsonage I was learning about being a holy woman of God on the inside, with new ways of looking heavenward. You can't be the companion of a spiritual man without reaching for that yourself. The things that had been theory to me, as I had read all those books about being a Christian woman, were now needing to be acted upon. Day to day, moment by moment, I was learning to lean on and trust in God for guidance and correction.

1 Peter 3:5 talks of the holy women of old "who hoped in God." They are a model for us, according to this verse. The whole passage, verses 1 through 8 at least (although the entire chapter is relevant), has the secrets to a happy, holy married life hidden in it. Let's see if we can find some of it—although it may take a lifetime for us to fully plumb the depths! It is a treasure chest we can dip into over our entire lives.

For in this way in former times the holy women also, who hoped in God, used to adorn themselves, being submissive to their own husbands; just as Sarah obeyed Abraham, calling him lord, and you have become her children if you do what is right without being frightened by any fear.

You husbands in the same way, live with your wives in an understanding way, as with someone weaker, since she is a woman; and show her honor as a fellow heir of the grace of life, so that your prayers will not be hindered.

To sum up, all of you be harmonious, sympathetic, brotherly, kindhearted, and humble in spirit.... 1 Peter 3:5-8 (NASB)

It is interesting that these verses talk about fear. In the beginning of a second marriage, there is naturally some fear. Being burned in the past, we tend to protect ourselves and hold back giving ourselves completely, *in case it is not going to last.* We don't want to be devastated if this is not as good as it seems. This is somewhat true even in first marriages, if one mate feels betrayed by the other but they have reconciled. We can resist putting our all into the marriage for fear of getting hurt again. I think the husbands do the same. It really gets down to whether we can trust *God* with our future, not whether the person or the marriage will be what we hope it is. Giving the relationship our all, and letting God protect us, is the secret to building or rebuilding trust.

That really applies to other areas of life too, not just marriage—do we fear that our boss, neighbor, parent, will let us down? Do we hold back from being close with people? I had to recognize fear and reject it, committing again to trust in God. He had, really and truly, shown me so many ways that He actually *was* in control, that it was reasonable that I should trust him when fears arose.

Fear works both ways too. If we are not leaning on God, and not letting Him soften us and give us wisdom, tolerance and forgiveness, our fears can cause us to react badly or try to control things, causing those around us to fear *us*. Too often others can tiptoe around us if they don't want to have to deal with us. They can fear our reactions, so it gets easier for them to not communicate about issues. Communication is so vital to good relationships that if fear is causing a strangling of thoughts or ideas between us, we definitely need to root out that fear. Like Sarah and the holy women of old, let us "do what is right without being frightened by any fear." It is right to reverence and love our husbands, and to do all we can to fulfill our role as his companion, comforter, and protector. We need to pour ourselves into this noble calling, and banish any fear.

> Then we turned and set out for the wilderness by the way to the Red Sea, as the LORD spoke to me, and circled Mount Seir for many days. And the LORD spoke to me, saying, 'You have circled this mountain long enough. Now turn north, and command the people, saying, "You will pass through the territory of your brothers the sons of Esau who live in Seir; and they will be afraid of you. So be very careful; do not provoke them, for I will not give you any of their land, even as little *as* a footstep because I have given Mount Seir to Esau as a possession." You shall buy food from them with money so that you may eat, and you shall also purchase water from them with money so that you may drink. For the LORD your God has blessed you in all that you have done; He has known your wanderings through this great wilderness. These forty years the LORD your God has been with you; you have not lacked a thing.' (Deuteronomy 2:1-8 KJV)

The Israelites were told by God "Do not provoke them, for I will not give you any of their land, even as little as a footstep because I have given Mount Seir to Esau as a possession." Now Esau was not the blessed son, and his clan did not follow God's ways; yet God asked Israel to *respect their territory*. It is interesting that God said, "they will be afraid of you. So be very careful, do not *provoke* them." Application for us holy (heavenly) women: Sometimes our husbands (and others in our lives) do not do what we think is the right thing, or they treat us in a way that we think is not fair or good. Maybe they *don't use the right tone*. Even so, if we react in the flesh rather than in a spiritual way, they may fear us and they also react in the flesh. If we *provoke* them, we may find ourselves with lots of hostility, or at least a breakdown of the gentle love we desire. My resident minister, though very spiritual, was human too, and if we were having a disagreement and I didn't like his tone, I would let it stoke fear in *me* that our wonderful love would not last. I think fear would enter his mind too, and silence and coldness could come between us until we couldn't stand it. We finally found ways to work through it to restore the closeness. So, I had to be careful of my reactions, careful that I didn't threaten to take over the man's territory and cause fear. Their territory can be their leadership, even their right to lead the family.

Go back to 1 Peter 3:1-8. There could be another entire library written on the whole misunderstood area of submission to husbands, so let's slide over that today. Let's look at some of the other practical ways that the Bible describes our model, "the holy women of old." By the way, when it mentions Sarah, and we shouldn't think of an old prune-faced crone; let's think mature super model. Read what Abraham says to Sarah in Genesis:

> It came about when he came near to Egypt, that he said to Sarai his wife, "See now, I know that you are a beautiful woman.... (Genesis 12:11 NASB)

Sarah was 65 at the time! Then it happens again when Sarah is about 90! She was beautiful and desirable as a woman; but that is beside the point here in 1 Peter. I just wanted you to know that holy women don't have to be plain and unattractive.

Look at this verse in 1 Peter, both in the Message and the King James Version:

> The same goes for you wives: Be good wives to your husbands, responsive to their needs. There are husbands who, indifferent as they are to any words about God, will be captivated by your life of holy beauty. What matters is not your outer appearance—the styling of your hair, the jewelry you wear, the cut of your clothes—but your inner disposition. (1 Peter 3:3,4 MSG)

> Likewise, ye wives, be in subjection to your own husbands; that, if any obey not the word, they also may without the word be won by the conversation of the wives;

> While they behold your chaste conversation coupled with fear.

> Whose adorning let it not be that outward adorning of plaiting the hair, and of wearing of gold, or of putting on of apparel ... (1 Peter 3,4 KJV)

This last verse has caused many devout women to neglect their outer appearance, thinking it means we shouldn't braid our hair or wear jewelry. If that was what it really is meaning, then we must also go naked, for the next phrase is literally "putting on dresses." The adornment should not be *merely* external; the emphasis is that we can't trust that our external beauty will be enough to do the trick, so to speak. A man loves to look at his beautiful wife, but even more, he wants to nearly worship her goodness. A man really does want a good wife, one he really respects. If he knows she is good and kind within, he will be far more willing to treat her with honor.

Still dissecting the 1 Peter 3 passage, we see another facet of how the holy women conduct themselves:

> Cultivate inner beauty, the gentle, gracious kind that God delights in. The holy women of old were beautiful before God that way, and were good, loyal wives to their husbands. Sarah, for instance, taking care of Abraham, would address him as "my dear husband." You'll be true daughters of Sarah if you do the same, unanxious and unintimidated. (1 Peter 3:5,6 MSG)

Some translations of 1 Peter say that Sarah was *respectful.* In the instances that we don't agree with our husbands or leaders or bosses, if we want to be like the holy women of old, we need to remind ourselves to be respectful. If the President of the United States comes to our town and we get to meet him, even if he is of another political persuasion, if we are civil people we would show respect on account of the office. That doesn't mean that wives cannot disagree, but if we want to be a heavenly woman, we should teach ourselves how to speak respectfully. The Bible says the husband is head of the wife, so if we want to be heavenly women, we need to respect the office God has assigned him, no matter if we think he is doing the job well or not. That is up to God, actually. And God knows him better than we do, and knows just how to head him off at the pass if he is going the wrong direction. It is so important for us both to let God do His work, while we do our work by being respectful, patient and loving.

Don't just respect his office, but remember to keep your love for him in your hearts, and be on his team. After all, that's the "Golden Rule" that Jesus gave us, to "Do unto others as you would have done unto you." When we have a fault that we are working on, or a past miss-step that we are sorry for, do we want our husband (or others) to continue to hold it against us or make us feel unloved because of it? No, we want them to love us unconditionally, cheering us on as we struggle to be better. It would be crushing if they just wrote us off as never possibly being what they want.

Since Thomas and I were newlyweds, it was natural to want to address him like Sarah did, "my dear husband." We need to keep that attitude when our honeymoon transitions to blending two different worlds. For instance: when in-laws enter the new marital bliss.

I had to learn the hard way. Sometime later in our first year together, in the heat of summer, we traveled from the North to the South where my extended family lived. Thomas would meet "the family," a huge clan of happy, loud, game-playing, watermelon seed-spitting, picnic-loving, falling-into-the-river relatives. Enter one quiet, proper, non-swimming Englishman whose very calling was enhanced by his love for books, libraries, contemplation, prayer, and serious conversation, with meals preferably cleanly indoors with napkins.

Not knowing what was in store, he agreed to an afternoon picnicking at a river. While my family and I enjoyed hours in the river, he tried to find shade to keep his English skin from burning, but the only shade he could find included mosquitoes, chiggers and ticks. When the rest of us were water-weary and exhausted, my mom and dad pulled picnic baskets from the 100 degree pickup trucks, and we feasted on delicious burned-black hot dogs, soft white buns, warm potato salad, and watermelon, with an unsettling sprinkling of flies landing on anything left uncovered for one minute. Trying to be as gracious as he could, Thomas didn't say much and tried to eat. The next day promised to be hotter yet, and Daddy suggested another trip to the river to cool off. Thomas said he would rather stay home—and I was really upset. How could he not try harder to fit in? I wanted so much for my family to admire him like I did, but I was sure they, especially my Daddy, would think he was odd if he stayed behind as we all went to have fun. We had what was probably our first argument, and I surely did not call him "my dear husband," like Sarah of old.

I was certain that I knew what he should do, and I was livid that he disagreed. I stormed and sulked, and he just clammed up and said he would spend the day at the library while we swam. I told him that we had to do what Daddy wanted, and it would be weird for him to not go along with it. In our family, everybody did what Daddy said. He was the "patriarch!" Finally, Thomas said quietly, "You have to decide whether you are first my wife, or your Daddy's little girl." I realized that I needed to respect his different choices, to set him free to be himself and not have to be exactly what my Daddy expected him to be. I had to respect who he was, as different as it might be from the world I grew up in. After all, he was not requiring me to stay behind and go to the library; he just wanted me to offer him the same courtesy of choice, with no anger or manipulation. How much better if I could have taken a page from Sarah's book, and said, *"My dear husband*, I am so glad that you encourage me to spend time with my wild country family, and it would be more fun for me if you were with me; but I do see that it is just fine if you take a quiet day off from the wildly chaotic river picnic."

Really, it is just basic respect for the other person, allowing them freedom, with no condemnation or manipulation. Sarah knew it, and now we do too!

LIVING IT:

This week, do not neglect your feminine outer beauty, but concentrate on beautifying your inner person. Try respect, civility, and soft, endearing words. Think back to words and attitudes of honeymoon time, if you are married.

FOR FUN:

Think hard about the preferences of those in your life. What do *they* want to do or eat? Is there comfort food from their past that you could make or buy as a sweet surprise, one that says, "You are dear to me"? Isn't it fun to concentrate on others' desires and comforts, as the secret heavenly woman you are becoming?

Chapter 8

THE COMFORTING WOMAN:
QUEEN OF HEARTH AND HOME

Our first parsonage was very nice, even if it was the church's and not mine, and I settled in happily. Over the years, I learned to consider it a real adventure when we frequently moved into a new one. Moving Day with the Methodist church was an incredible musical-chair thing. Because of the itinerant nature of the Methodist ministry, many pastors change churches and parsonages frequently, and to make it work, they all move on the same "moving day" each year. The outgoing pastor's family packs all their lives into a moving van in the morning, cleans the house to make it ready for the incoming pastor, and drives to the new church assignment in the afternoon to unload their books and clothing and furniture and kids and their dog into the new assignment. Thomas also had to pack up his church office, unpack that into a new church office, meet the committees and boards and staff, as well as the little thing of preparing his first sermon to be delivered to a new congregation looking for a perfect new minister. No stress there!

Usually the new congregation would bring supper for us, which was so welcome, with all our dishes still somewhere in boxes. The church was putting its best foot forward, as were we.

One such moving day, as we arrived to our first church in the South, we got a phone call as we were unloading the moving van. The woman said she and her husband were bringing us "possum pie," and they would love to eat it with us. We graciously thanked them—what else could we do?—but as we awaited their arrival, we panicked. *Possum pie? Ew.* We were Northerners who had never ever seen a possum pie. It turned out that the couple was only teasing and actually brought a beautiful chocolate pie. Their joke lightened a tiring day, and they became good friends.

Another moving day something happened that wasn't funny, but was a true God-thing, and a teaching lesson for me. To back up, Thomas had been working on his undergraduate degree, and to pay for tuition, we raised Irish Setter puppies. It so happened that when moving day came, our pups were just 5 weeks old and not old enough to sell, so we had our two mama setters, our daddy setter, and about 20 pups. What to do? We had never even seen the new parsonage, which was two hours away from our old one, and we hoped there would be a yard big enough for them. I was nervous about what the parsonage committee's reaction would be to the Beverly Hillbillies arriving with a pickup truck, three doghouses and 101 Dalmatians. But I had a lesson to learn about worrying. God is so good. He had arranged that the head of the parsonage committee was a great dog lover herself who actually raised *Irish Setters!* The doggies got a warm welcome and lots of hugs! She also became a wonderful friend, and I learned how God prepares the way. When I start to be anxious about what others will think, I often remember how God worked the dog situation out perfectly.

We moved a lot as our pulpits got shuffled at the District Superintendents' meetings, and after a while I got used to the routine. Thomas and some of the church members would unload our moving van at the new parsonage, then drive it to the church to unload his books and office things, leaving me to turn what looked like a box warehouse into a place to "camp" for the night—at least a place to sleep and eat. First job, of course, was finding the boxes marked "open me first" for bedding, bathroom items, clothing for tomorrow and immediate kitchen items for breakfast. The first night we all just crashed. The next morning, after Thomas went to the church (he was expected to start running the church on day two!), I started to turn the parsonage into our home.

Having all my own furniture and pictures made it seem like home pretty quickly, although it took longer to get all the boxes unpacked. My aim was to make it seem comforting and familiar, a safe haven in a new situation. I delighted in seeing how my husband would like it when he came home that first day from the church office—what a change one day could make! I tried to help the children see it as an adventure too, letting them pick their bedrooms and adjust the decor for them. It was even more fun when I had things straightened out enough to take time to explore the new village or city with the children, looking especially for fun or interesting places we could put on our "field trips" list in our homeschooling.

How often have I heard women complain that they just hate the town they had to move to for their husband's good promotion, or they don't like the house, or the climate, or whatever. Having a positive frame of mind makes such a difference, and if we *look for the good,* and seek out the little gifts that God has supplied in the situation, we will be further along on our journey to becoming heavenly women. We will be happier, and since we have such woman power, it is contagious.

We read in earlier chapters about one of the "holy woman of old," Sarah. Her husband, Abraham, was told by God to pick up and leave their home and travel across the deserts to a place God would show him. Sarah had to trust that her husband had heard God, and she went where he led:

> Now the LORD said to Abram, "Go forth from your country, And from your relatives And from your father's house, To the land which I will show you. (Genesis 12:1 NASB)

Sometimes God speaks to our husbands, but not to us, and we have to just trust God that He has it all under control, especially if we are concerned that the direction sounds odd. I have found that if I pray about it, God usually gives me confirmation that even though it may not be a convenient direction, it is indeed the one He has in mind. There have been times that the direction doesn't turn out the way we hoped, but we didn't doubt that God had led us. The direction we took had a lesson for us to learn, or a special situation that Thomas was able to minister to, after which He directed us in a different direction. So, it all boils down to trusting God.

It is important, through all this, to be able to communicate clearly and respectfully with our spouses. I know it is ok to say, "I am not seeing that this is a good direction to go; however, I will pray about it." If I get confirmation, that helps my husband to feel confident to go ahead. If I pray and still have reservations, I owe it to him to tell him, respectfully; then he has to go back to God and ask if he heard right. If he still is sure, then I give it over to God, because I know He always has the long view and his own purposes, so I can have peace. I learned that my attitude needed to be one of cooperation and communication, then trust.

The important thing for a woman who would like to be more heavenly is to have a good attitude:

> for it is God who works in you to will and to act in order to fulfill his good purpose.
>
> Do everything without grumbling [complaining] or arguing, so that you may become blameless and pure, "children of God without fault in a warped and

crooked generation." Then you will shine among
them like stars in the sky. (Philippians 2:13-15 NIV)

Do we want to shine like stars in the sky? Or maybe another
thing from above:

A quarrelsome wife is like the constant dripping of
a leaky roof. (Proverbs 9:13 NIV)

Speaking of a roof over a home, a heavenly woman tries to
keep the home "dry and comfortable," a place the family wants
to return to. It is a sacred and high calling to be the Queen of the
Home, no matter what the modern culture says about it.

In *The One Life Dream That Makes a Girl Blush,* Andrea
Burke wrote about a counseling session she was having with a
teenage girl:

"I know it's silly," one girl said. "I know. But..."--she
hesitated, tucking a strand of hair behind her ear. "I
really just want to be married. To raise some kids.
To take care of a home." She's almost embarrassed
by the time she's finished saying the sentiment. As
if admitting it has made any impressive strength
and wit she had fade away into a pile of proverbial
laundry and dishes. As if she's ashamed for wanting
something so 'trivial' and simple. "Is that silly? I
mean, it's really all I really want to do."

Our modern culture has taught girls that if they are going to
amount to something, it has to be "out there," in a career. If they
aspire to do what women have done for centuries, to love being
in their own home bringing up their own babies, they are to be
pitied. Yet the crushing statistics of failed marriages and suicidal
teens should make us all stop and question whether the modern
idea for women is really better, after all, for the home and the
family. Women have every right to have careers if that is what

they want for *their own* fulfillment. But how does that fulfill the *husband and children?*

> This is what the LORD says: Stand at the crossroads and look; ask for the ancient paths, ask where the good way is, and walk in it, and you will find rest for your souls. But you said, 'We will not walk in it.' (Jeremiah 6:16 NIV)

The picture some people want to paint of a stay-at-home Christian woman is something like Cinderella, wearing rags and scrubbing floors. But that's looking at the glass half empty instead of half full. It would be more accurate to see the Christian stay-at-home woman as Cinderella *after* the pixie dust adorned her in that amazing gown, and the prince chose her at the ball, and she became queen of the palace.

The heavenly woman has a realm all of her own! The saying goes that a man is king of his castle; if so even more, the wife is queen of her home. His castle, as a lot of people refer to his home, is a lot bigger than the home. It includes his profession, his feeling of self-worth as leader of the family, the responsibility to guide his family, his headship of the relationships of his family, his financial kingdom, his barn and shed and garage and lawn and tractor and saws and his dog—much more than just a house. In England, Thomas and I visited a beautiful castle, where the grounds and stables and granaries and businesses were all within the castle walls. The actual dwelling of the lord and lady of the castle was just a part of it, their own residence.

But the house itself—ah, that is our domain. The Bible says that we should be "keepers of the home." Young's Literal Translation of Titus 2:5 says women should be "sober, pure, keepers of their own houses...." The Greek Word is *oikourous*. The etymology of this word suggests the meaning "house-keeper" (*oikos* = house + ouros = keeper, watcher, or guardian.) Sadly, our current culture has demoted "housekeeper" to an uneducated hired helper.

Some of the earliest Greek manuscripts have a slightly different word *oikodespoteō,* which has the connotation of *supervising the servants* in the home! Sounds better all the time! Ok, most of us don't have servants. Oh wait—we do. I read somewhere that our modern appliances are equivalent to seven servants in Bible times. Although I am not rich by any stretch of the imagination, I actually have a robot vacuum/mop, dishwasher, clothes washer and dryer, instant oven, bread machine, microwave, instant pot, running water, water heater, sewing machine, refrigerator, freezer, automatic furnace and air conditioner—the list goes on. Imagine how many Bible times servant jobs that would cover just to keep a home running! How can we not have a grateful attitude as we keep a good house for our husband and children? We should not ever look down on the traditional job women have done for thousands of years without any of the things that we have to help us.

> Guide older women into lives of reverence so they end up as neither gossips nor drunks, but models of goodness. By looking at them, the younger women will know how to love their husbands and children, be virtuous and pure, keep a good house, be good wives. We don't want anyone looking down on God's Message because of their behavior. (Titus 2:2-5 NIV)

When we are getting ready to marry, most of us think we have found Prince Charming himself. I remember one of my sisters describing the man she had just gotten engaged to: "I know that you think I'm prejudiced because I'm engaged to him, but he really *is* perfect." A year later, she told me half jokingly she would give him to anyone. Of course, that is pretty normal—that first year when you find Mr. Charming has a few faults, you have to reconcile your romantic fantasies with real life. (She did adapt, and they lived a long happy marriage together, and raised lovely children, most of them in some kind of Christian ministry.)

I was thinking of the old tune, "After the ball is over...." OK, so Mr. Charming, after the ball, may not always act very princely. Sometimes he has bad days. He has character flaws, as we all do, that he is—or hopefully will be—working on. But no matter, you are queen, not only because Prince Charming chose you, but even more, because the King of the Universe has chosen you. He has called you to be His. You will be able to be "keeper, watcher, guardian" of this realm He has bestowed on you. And you won't have to do it alone: He promises to be your *helper!* I found that amazing: the Bible said I was to be a "helper" for my husband, and now I read that *my* "helper" is God Himself! If He will do that for me, I surely can do that for my sometimes not-so-charming earthly prince!

Devi Titus, author of "Home Experience," says the heart is formed in the home. The home is our sanctuary. Dignity and sanctity reign if we invite the Prince of Peace into our home, and the home is where we as women are queens who birth and nurture a civilization with a heart.

The great classic studied in most universities, *The Rise and Fall of the Roman Empire*, lists the reasons civilizations crumble. If you can believe it, the author lists as number one: "the loss of the dignity and sanctity of the home." Dignity of the home is lost when all schools talk about to little girls is the many ways they can get out of it and into a "fulfilling" career—none of that vapid 50's, "Leave it to Beaver" life for them! "You can be anything you want to be" is their mantra. The demise of the family home is the goal of the enemy of our souls and the deceiver of our hearts. He is the very one who has engineered the fall of mankind and who designs chaos and misery for us all, culminating, if he can arrange it, an eternity with him in Dante's inferno.

Think about it: the sanctity of the home is lost when society desecrates the sanctuary of it. God sanctified the family unit, a man and a woman leaving their parents and joining together as a new family, bearing their children. Modern thinking is that any type of group that says it is a family is a family. We saw it begin in the 60's with the hippie communes, where droves of teens rebelled against their parents and traded their real family for a free-love commune. That was Pandora's Box, and now it has opened, and only time will tell the damage that has been done to the home.

President Reagan said the most important conversation in the world is the one at the family dinner table. You know the one—the thing in the 50's where dad comes home from work and the family gathers around a table to eat a balanced meal together and share their lives. Not the one of fast food eaten on the run, jammed between school and sports games or between shifts of mom and dad going to or coming from work and kids' activities.

Speaking of food, it is so much more than sustenance. Food has an important place in making a house into a home. Ah, comfort food! I have learned how to make English food since I married an Englishman. I can't complain about how that started: Thomas took me to England to meet the folks, which was an incredible trip. I got to see firsthand how he almost sighed when his mother served him "custard" over apple crumble, or bread pudding, or little English apple pies—and his pure delight at fish and chips eaten out of a newspaper cone as we walked the ancient cobbled streets.

The heavenly woman knows that her kitchen is not a place of drudge, as modern scoffers would have us believe, but a mysterious laboratory where she conjures up more woman power. She has her own version of pixie dust that changes protein and carbs into sighs of satisfaction. She is building up her home with her own hands. The old time women used to say to the young ones, "The way to a man's heart is through his stomach." I might add that the way *home* is through the stomach. We want our man and our children to be drawn to the home in every way we can. The home as a place of safety and peace is reinforced by the comfort food we are smart enough to provide.

> The wise woman builds her house, But the foolish
> tears it down with her own hands. (Proverbs 14:1
> NASB)

Speaking of "with her own hands," I learned to make bread, partly for the health benefits, but also to add that incomparable and wonderful aroma of baking bread to my heavenly domain! I used to knead it with my own hands, but now I use my own bread machine "hands," and the aroma and taste are just as wonderful. It may be just a little thing, but it sets the tone as soon as the family member opens the door.

Left to my natural tendencies, I confess that in housekeeping, I'm a "messie." That term came from the book *The Messie's Manual,* by Sandra Felton. Early in our marriage, Thomas and I were browsing in a bookstore, and I was standing there looking through the book. Thomas came up beside me and said, humorously, he thought, "It will take more than a book for you." He didn't mean it to hurt, for we had joked about how different we were about neatness. But something in me *saw* for the first time, that it wasn't a laughing matter. I realized that I was not really trying to be a heavenly woman in the area of housekeeping, because I just said I was a "casual" housekeeper. We bought the book, and it really was a turnaround for me. *Read it if you dare!* Sandra talks of her own wake-up call when she *saw* herself as what she was, a "messie." And she designed ways to help get the home under her control so it went from messy chaos to peaceful order. Her ideas kick-started me in the right direction, and I have really enjoyed the difference. So did Thomas and the children! I am the "natural" style type, and will never be as neat as the "classic" type. We are all different, but none of us should settle for dirt and disorder.

Once I could finally find things and discard junk and have a "sorta" schedule to keep it clean, I could enjoy dreaming of ways to make it beautiful. One way was to use "my" colors, and

I found that using our own color palette brings harmony and beauty even to inexpensive furnishings. Not only that, when my home is decorated in colors I love, then I love my home. When I love my home, it is contagious; the others in the family love it too. They might not want to decorate their homes like I do, and they might use different colors, but they see my home as an extension of *me*. I lived in parsonages, so for me, the addition of accent colors and temporary fixes had to do, but still it worked. I would look through home magazines and save any pictures I loved in a folder that was helping me to develop my own style. Sometimes just having our dreams in a folder is enough, since in life we have to be patient. Many years later, now that we are retired from the church ministry and have our own home, I dug out my favorite kitchen picture of all time, and had it built in my cottage home! I actually now live in my childhood dream of a rose-covered cottage. No picket fence, but a beautiful rock wall is even better! Good things come to those who wait!

A wise heavenly woman makes her home a place of beauty, peace, and comfort, with lots of food and warmth and happiness!

LIVING IT:

Make your home a sanctuary for *your* soul, as well as for others in your family. Things you can change easily: add soft music, good aromas, flowers. Smiles are another easy addition. Wear everyday things that you love. Pray as you go about your home.

A husband and children need a clean home, well-managed meals, clean clothes, and a content, happy Queen. The wife herself actually feels better too with a clean home, well-managed meals, clean clothes and *being* content and happy, so we should do it for ourselves as well as for them. If your home needs to run more smoothly, here are some ideas of what can you do to organize:

- Menus—try writing out your family's favorite menus enough for two weeks. Once that is done, you can use it again and again! You will amaze your family! When you know what you will be serving ahead of time, you have time to make do-ahead things like boiled eggs for the salad and Jell-O salad for dessert, and can have a fairly standard shopping list too.
- Shopping—make a careful shopping list with your menus in front of you, and avoid impulse buying. Keep items stored ahead, and add it to your shopping list when you pull your reserve item into use so you never run out of anything. Buying ahead when things are on sale saves money too!
- Laundry—take charge of supervising it, even if other family members help. This is too important to let chaos reign! And putting away is part of the job too. Let your children know you love folding laundry and having neat storage, and they will learn to enjoy it too.
- Cleaning—you can list jobs that need done weekly and decide which should be done on which days, then try to stick to it until it is routine. Of course, other family members can do some of the work, but as Queen, you should reign over it all.

FOR FUN:

Try the 5-minute cleaning blitz: Set the timer for 5 minutes and see how many things you can pick up or put away or straighten or wipe or sweep in one room for just 5 minutes. Then make yourself stop and move on to another room and repeat. Think how much fresher your home will look in just 30 minutes!

Chapter 9

THE SPIRIT-FILLED WOMAN—
RUNNING ON EMPTY
OR BEING FILLED

The Bible says that there is a season for everything: "A time to weep and a time to laugh; A time to mourn and a time to dance." (Ecclesiastes 3:4) After years of sadness and rejection, my first years as "minister's wife" were full of joy, as the children were young and so was my new love and my new role. I was learning new ways of living, putting into practice new habits of Christian motherhood and wife-hood, loving the adventure of the ministry, even the moving from parish to parish. I was enjoying the season of "a time to dance." Not literally, although my Resident Minister and I did enjoy an occasional quiet waltz to soft music and candlelight after the children were asleep. I was learning to "keep" house better too, so that our home was more peaceful and comforting than I had ever known, and we had years of "a time to laugh."

Thomas urged me to use that golden time to build up my faith, and he diligently and gently led me in growth. He very kindly told me that my spirit needed nourishment, something I had never even thought of. He read the scriptures to me before bedtime, and in the morning at breakfast. It was a pure delight to me, something I had not experienced in marriage before: a man bearing the burden of bringing his household into godly order, leading me in spiritual growth. He showed me that Jesus said you have to build before the storm comes:

> Therefore everyone who hears these words of Mine and acts on them, may be compared to a wise man who built his house on the rock. And the rain fell, and the floods came, and the winds blew and slammed against that house; and yet it did not fall, for it had been founded on the rock. Everyone who hears these words of Mine and does not act on them, will be like a foolish man who built his house on the sand. The rain fell, and the floods came, and the winds blew and slammed against that house; and it fell—and great was its fall. (Matthew 7:24-27, NASB)

In his ministry, Thomas had seen so many people who had not taken time for God until their lives fell apart; then they had no foundation to fall back on, so even though God came to their rescue, they had a much harder time of it. He gave me cassette tapes (shows you how long ago that was!) of great Bible teachings that I could play as I went about my housework. Sometimes he read portions to me from whatever current Christian book he was reading, and we had lots of discussion of the meaning and practice of the Christian faith. Nightly, we knelt together by the sofa and prayed for our family, our parishioners, etc. I kept a journal of the answers to prayers, and sometimes I get old journals out and marvel as I read them over and remember. We still get answers to prayer, but in that "season" it was almost like a honeymoon with God, getting surprising and amazing and encouraging answers!

I basked in the golden glow. My young children were playing

in the sunshine, we were enjoying home-schooling, my husband was having happy congregations, and he was working on his graduate degrees. There was a little plaque on my wall that I had painted, showing a mother and little girl in a rocking chair that said,

> Cleaning and scrubbing can wait 'til tomorrow
> For babies grow up we've learned to our sorrow,
> So quiet down cobwebs and dust go to sleep
> I'm rocking my baby, and babies don't keep.
> --Ruth Hulburt Hamilton

I thought it was just a sweet poem. The part about babies growing up seemed to be in the distant misty future, as my days were full of laughter and fun and food and I thought it would go on for years.

But years do slip by, and before I knew it, I had teenagers. Teenager trials can be multiplied during the breakup of a marriage and the building of a new one, and we were finding it challenging. The shards of my earlier life seemingly were glued and patched together now, but in the children, the cracks were still there, causing pain unknown to me. Our beautiful 16-year-old daughter, who had always been so easy to have around, was going through what I now know is normal teenage times of trying to find her own way in life. And Thomas and I were just learning to be parents of teenagers, doing most of it wrong! When I was talking to a wise old lady in our church about handling teenagers, (I thought she was old then, but she was probably twenty years younger than I am now!) she just laughed and said, "Oh, didn't you know that kids take 'stupidity pills' from about 16 to 26?" That lightened it up for me somewhat.

In the Matthew 7 scripture verses above, notice verse 25 says, "the rain fell, and the floods came, and the winds slammed against that house." Not "*if* the rains fall, and *if* the floods come, and *if* the winds blow and slam against the house," but that they *will* come. I just didn't know that meant *my* house.

My slamming storm came in the form of a note I found on the island in the kitchen one sunny afternoon as I returned from the grocery store. "I'm sorry, I have to do this." *Do what?* I went to my daughter's room, but she wasn't there. She wasn't anywhere in the house or on the property. She didn't drive yet and didn't have a car. Shock set in as I realized she had run away. Talk about a storm hitting me—the buckets of tears I had cried over my marriage breakup were nothing to the deluge of the next few weeks of our not knowing where she was or what was happening to her. Pictures of missing children on milk cartons had meant nothing to me before; never again would I be able to look at one without feeling great empathy for the parents of that missing child.

I went through weeks of despondency. I could not believe this was happening to me, to us. We did everything we could to find her. She was gone and seemingly had vanished without a trace. We prayed, we fasted, we searched. I tried to "be strong," to "have faith," and all those good things. I tried to be cheerful, to look for the good, to bear up beautifully. But I failed. I came up empty. I found that I didn't have the strength I thought I should. What about the scripture that if we built our house before the storm, our house would not fall? My house certainly felt like it had collapsed. Where was my faith? Where was God? We were the minister's family, and we had tried to do all we were supposed to. (In the storm, we can often blame others for our pain—there was plenty of blame to go around, I saw later.) How could this happen to us? Actually, God was getting ready to teach me that bad things are part of life and part of our faith walk. All is not sunshine, after all. Time to grow up, time to learn to live peacefully in sun or storm.

One morning after another crying night, I just didn't want

to get up. I was done. I turned my face toward the wall, like Hezekiah of old.

> 'Set your house in order, for you shall die and not live.' Hezekiah turned his face to the wall and prayed to the LORD, and said, "Remember now, O LORD, I beseech You, how I have walked before You in truth and with a whole heart, and have done what is good in Your sight." And Hezekiah wept bitterly.
>
> Then the word of the LORD came to Isaiah, saying, "Go and say to Hezekiah, 'Thus says the LORD, the God of your father David, "I have heard your prayer, I have seen your tears...." (Isaiah 38:1-5 NASB)

Thomas encouraged me to ask for a fresh filling of the Holy Spirit, since Jesus promised to send us the Holy Spirit as our comforter and helper. Since I was completely empty, I didn't think I had the faith to "be filled," as the Bible instructs us:

> Be filled with the Spirit, speaking to one another in psalms and hymns and spiritual songs, singing and making melody with your heart to the Lord....
> Ephesian 5:18 (NASB)

I thought it meant I needed to have the spiritual strength to reach out and get filled and sing and make melody in my heart, out of *true grit*. I just wanted to give up, feeling that I had nothing in *myself*.

Then one of those revelation moments happened: I *saw* that the filling was something that would be done *to* me, not *by* me, if I just opened my empty heart to the Lord so *He* could fill it. I reached out to God, and said something like, "I just can't do this, Lord. I need help. Please fill me with your Holy Spirit." Here is an amazing thing: He did. Immediately, I felt a little spark of joy somewhere in my soul. A little spring in the desert started up, and a little song started to faintly make melody in my heart! Peace and joy came to me. I knew I was going to live and not die. I got up, and my attitude was all different. And it was nothing I had "gumption'd" up; it was all the Holy Spirit of God!

Especially when the storms are slamming against your house, and faithfulness and peace and joy eludes you, it is good to recall that we never *were* that great in ourselves. But we have a great and compassionate God, and He says if we are filled with His Holy Spirit, He will provide all these things. Trying to conjure up these on our own is like gluing fake apples onto an apple tree; we need to just let the Holy Spirit grow the fruit in us. It is His own fruit that we need:

> But the fruit of the Spirit is love, joy, peace, patience, kindness, goodness, faithfulness, gentleness, self-control.... (Galatians 5:22, NASB)

The one lesson I learned through all that was how simple it is to believe, to have access to God and His promises. All any of us has to do when we are overwhelmed, when we can't find the faith we need, is to admit that in ourselves we are bankrupt, and turn to Jesus, our Savior. He promises to deliver us!

> Are you tired? Worn out? Burned out on religion? Come to me. Get away with me and you'll recover your life. I'll show you how to take a real rest. Walk with me and work with me—watch how I do it. Learn the unforced rhythms of grace. I won't lay anything heavy or ill-fitting on you. Keep company with me and you'll learn to live freely and lightly. (Matthew 11:28-30 MSG)

I'm sure you will want to know that my daughter and I got through that rough patch and she became a lovely mother of four children and is one of the nicest people you could know. (Remember, teenage years are filled with tumultuous emotions and confusion for both child and parents, about goals and roles—but they too pass!) God helped me instantly at the time I was overwhelmed, and He has taught me a lot about how He loves and cares for me and mine, and about how in His own time, and in His own way, He works things out.

LIVING IT:

We don't have to wait until storms hit to ask for God's amazing Helper, the Holy Spirit. He says it is for all of us, for all time! See Acts 3:28,29: "You will receive the gift of the Holy Spirit. For the promise is for you and your children and for all who are far off, as many as the Lord our God will call." (KJV) Remember, you don't need strength on your own. Just ask! He is ready to help you!

FOR FUN:

This was a heavy chapter. Take a break, lighten up, and do something enjoyable this week. Take a little time to shop, if you love that, or read a book and eat chocolate, or whatever sounds delightful. God is a great Father; think how much joy we get in taking our little children or grandies to a zoo or McDonalds, and imagine what joy God gets in seeing you, His dear child, enjoying His delights.

Here is another fun thing to make memorizing something hard very easy. I had tried for years to memorize the "fruits of the spirit" list from Galatians 5: Love, Joy, Peace, Patience, Kindness, Goodness, Faithfulness, Gentleness, and Self-control. I am not a great memorizer, but I read a book once about how to memorize by word pictures in your brain, and I found that this works. The idea is to think of ridiculous action pictures associated with the first letter of each listed word, in a sequence, and since they are so unusual, the brain remembers them. In this instance, I was talking with my little grandchildren about memorizing the fruits of the spirit, and to illustrate how to do the word picture thing, I said, "Picture in your head Little Jeweled Princesses Pushing Kids; Go Fast, Go Slow." I grabbed a piece of paper and scribbled a huge chair (to set the size) and at the floor by the bottom of the chair leg, three tiny princesses (Snow White, Cinderella, and Belle) with huge crowns on their heads with sparkly diamonds on them. I drew their hands pushing baby carriages and drew a little kid standing in each of the carriages. Then I drew a road sign that said "GO FAST," and then a stop sign that said "GO SLOW." My grandchildren giggled at the silliness of it, but each, in turn, recited the silly story and then the list of the fruits of the spirit. Even the seven-year-old got it immediately.

Chapter 10

THE PRAYING WOMAN—FROM THE NEST AND BEYOND

When my babies were small, I used to cuddle them and plant kisses on their chubby little necks, delighting in their sweet helplessness. My life had revolved around seeing that their round tummies were full of milk, that their clothes were clean and dry (including cloth diapers in those days), and that they were safe and protected and rocked. God puts that mother instinct into us that changes us forever when we become moms. We watch over our little nestlings with a fierceness and consuming love that we never knew before, and we want to be there for every new discovery, every new tooth, each amazing new word they learn.

I have fond memories of each baby's first spring as they took their first toddling steps on the soft grass in the sunshine. Their wonder at the new great outdoor world with singing birds, fluttering new green leaves on the trees, spring flowers in all colors—amazing things they had not seen in the long bitter northern winter—brought gurgles of delight.

I think that when we are new baby Christians, God delights in our discovery of His wonderful world, as He sets us in green pastures and leads us beside still waters. Every prayer brings miraculous answers, every word of The Word is a delight to our new eyes, and it seems life could not be better!

But that is babyhood. Real life, beyond the nest, is a dangerous place, and one that requires skill, knowledge, and strength to survive. God knows this and is the Master Gardener. My husband's hobby of growing plants yields delicate seedlings. He carefully replants them as they grow, avoiding crushing the fragile stems. He feeds and waters them every day, checking on their growth. When they grow bigger, the stems are a little stiffer and stronger, and he may move them each into a little bigger pot. One fine day, when the frosts are gone, but before the burning summer sun comes, he sets the pots outside in the shade to "harden off." They are no longer protected by the greenhouse, and maybe the plants wonder what has happened when the first downpour bends their heads down, and when that dries up and they get a little thirsty. Next, they get moved into the sunshine for a few days. Ouch! That is hot. And dry! And what are these little bugs that want to take a bite out of my leaves? Where is my greenhouse? Has my Gardener forgotten me? But no, here He is, taking me out of my pot and spreading my roots into a lovely, moist, rich place in His garden! I love it, and it feels so good to spread out my roots and drink the rain and soak up sunshine, and reach for the sky. Somehow I know now that I want to bear fruit, and I put all my energy into doing what I was designed for! The greenhouse is a distant memory of my babyhood, and now I am participating in God's rhythms of grace.

> Walk with me and work with me—watch how I do it. Learn the unforced rhythms of grace. (Matthew 11:29, MSG)

Psalm 23, verses 1 through 5, shows us the rhythms of grace in stages: first, our babyhood, in the nest:

The LORD is my shepherd,
I shall not want.
He makes me lie down in green pastures;
He leads me beside quiet waters.
He restores my soul;
He guides me in the paths of righteousness
For His name's sake. (NKJV)

Second, beyond the nest:

Even though I walk through the valley of the shadow
of death,
I fear no evil, for You are with me;
Your rod and Your staff, they comfort me.
You prepare a table before me in the presence of
my enemies;
You have anointed my head with oil;
My cup overflows. (NKJV)

So, the years of just basking in the golden glow of new marriage and young family times were sort of a *nest* time, strengthening me for what God had in mind for me: to be part of His prayer army. Yes, outside of the nest is a dangerous place, the valley of the shadow of death where evil lurks and God's discipline forms and comforts us; but we all do have to leave the nest. My children were growing up and would be leaving the home nest, and I too was growing up spiritually and would be leaving my golden nest. We would all have to face the downpours and scorching heat of the real world.

I had learned a lot of basics of what the Christian life was about, but looking back, I blush to realize my many failings in raising my children, in spite of all my efforts. Perhaps God used my failings to strengthen me; my errors were the downpours, the scorching sun, the bugs that bit my leaves. I was being hardened off, so I could be fruitful in His garden.

Just as the mother bird, at the right time, pushes the fledglings from the nest, and they learn to fly on their own, we helped our little feathered ones out, and they flew. I did the best I could with the understanding I had at the time, but now I wonder how scary and painful it was for them, and I wonder if they felt abandoned. I was also being pushed from my comfort-zone nest, needing to learn to fly on my own spiritual wings. I was learning that to fly without spiritual wings was to crash—my natural wings just didn't work in the valley downdrafts.

When children are little, we do pray for them, but the urgency for prayer is not there because *we* can *make* them do pretty much what we want. We are the giants in the room and they are little; they generally comply with our rules, whether we pray or not. I remember someone telling about their little son who was standing up in the backseat of the car, *in the day* before we had seat belts, and the father said, "Son, you have to sit down in the car." The little child didn't listen and remained standing, leaning against the front seat. The father said, "If you don't sit down, I'll have to stop the car and spank you." The little one plopped down on the seat, but said, "OK, I'm sitting down on the outside, but I'm standing up on the inside." No wonder that when the little ones become big teenagers, their little rebel attitudes spread from inside, where it had to stay when young, to the outside for all to see. That's when we parents really find an urgent need to pray. I know that's when I found myself praying harder than I ever had. And that was just teenager stuff! I had no idea then that when the children are grown and having their own children, going through divorces and job losses and all the things out there outside of the nest, with our having absolutely no say in what they do anymore, I would *really* pray.

About pushing the little birds out of the nest, I am chagrined to think of how the first one went. You've heard the term "poor as church mice;" well, we lived on what they called a student pastor salary for the years Thomas was finishing his graduate school, and we had no money to send our children to college. Our oldest, Andy, had always wanted to be a pilot. I figured that if he could get into the Air Force ROTC program, they would pay for his college, so I spent lots and lots of time and energy making that happen for him. He got accepted, and enrolled in a college in Arizona where one of my older sisters lived. She had invited him to live with her family, and his college costs were covered by the Air Force, so I figured it was time for him to leave the nest and fly. Literally. Anyway, we didn't have any vacation time from the church, and we had just the time between Sundays to get Andy to college. So, Thomas and I packed all the children in our old station wagon and headed off across the US, driving day and night, and got there in 3 days, unloaded Andy and his suitcase, and turned around and headed back East, arriving just in time for Thomas's Sunday sermon. That's all we could do. But that poor little bird had to not only get his bearings but do all the paperwork to get signed up for classes and get books and whatever else needed taken care of. He managed, and he did graduate with an electrical engineering degree, and he did go on to fly all over the world with the Air Force, so I guess the little bird used his wings and flew. Still, I wonder if he felt orphaned down inside. I wish we could have made it easier for him, but we were just learning too.

Kiddos #2 and #3 were dropped off at colleges similarly in their own turn, and we stayed with them slightly longer and helped with paperwork and places to stay and jobs; but the days in the nest were over, and from then on they flew on their own. Kid #4 had dreamed of building houses as his life work, although he was really fascinated by his uncle's little airplane too. He did a little community college work, but went directly into construction work, and on the side learned to fly and got his pilot license. So our nest was empty.

I had always thought that once the kids are grown and out of the nest, life would be easy. I hadn't thought about the momma bird probably hovering nervously as her little ones jump from the nest and either fly away or dash on the rocks below, and there isn't a thing she can do about it. So I prayed.

I prayed about their college work. One time son #2 called to say he was failing in a really challenging class, and his professor actually advised him to drop out, that he just didn't have what it takes. Imagine what Mama Bear advised! I told him to STAY and I would pray. I prayed with all that was within me! He passed that class, had other iffy ones; I prayed, he passed more. He is a veterinary surgeon now, and God gets the glory.

I prayed about their choice of mates. I prayed about their sticking with their choice of mates. It seemed that I prayed "to no avail," as I helplessly stood by and watched divorce shatter grandchildren's lives like I had seen it do to my children. But I had to trust that God was working out his own purposes in the grown kids' lives and that He would be working in the grandchildren's lives too. Trust means believing that He knows what it takes to help them grow strong, even if it is downpours and storms that smash the house.

I prayed shocked, terrified, panicky, all-consuming, desperate prayers when "that phone call" came that we all dread. Son #4, the aspiring home builder, had just the week before proudly shown us around his current job, a beautiful home in an exclusive mountainous village. The back of the house had a deck that perched over a seemingly bottomless chasm, with a wonderful view. He had joked that since he was the junior member of the crew, they gave him the jobs like crawling out over the canyon to attach whatever to whatever to construct the deck. Now it was an early morning, and the phone rang. I answered, and it was one of my sisters, sounding rather odd. She said she was sorry to tell us that he had fallen off a roof and was in St. Joseph's Hospital, and all she knew was he was "still alive." We drove the hour and a half through hills at speeds usually impossible, and I guarantee that you can pray intensely for an hour and a half! When we got there, he was stretched out on a table, still in his old work clothes, conscious but gasping for air, while they were looking at x-rays and deciding what to do. The image is so imprinted in my brain, that as I just typed the last line my eyes brimmed with tears, and it brought back how frightened and horrified I was—and that was 30-something years ago. Was I trusting God? Had I been praying? Yes, but it is reality to be mortified at the same time. The doctor showed us the x-rays with a spine broken in many places, and he said they would need to operate and put steel rods all along both sides of the spine. I moved into the hospital for several weeks to be with him as he recovered, as he couldn't do anything for himself. Then we took him home to live with us. It was a long recovery. He did go back to building somewhat, with limited lifting ability, but started doing more flying. Really flying, not just from the nest. Even today, years later, he still does woodworking and building things here and there, but mainly he is a jet pilot, which he loves. Who knows, maybe without the accident he might not have changed careers. Only God knows, and once they fly away, it is up to them and God to work out things. Still, I pray.

Life is full of great fun things and awful terrible things. This world is a hard place, and we are set down right in the middle of it, given the astounding and important work of altering the balance of powers by prayer. Ephesians 6:12 describes it as "heavenly places!" Maybe because we are aiming to be heavenly women, we are right there among it all, praying. We are praying all kinds of prayer: the terrified, pleading prayer after "the phone call," the insisting and logical prayer about staying on course as veterinary student, the agonized and heart-broken prayer for a child's dissolving marriage. Many kinds of prayers. As heavenly women, we are told to pray at all times in the Spirit, with all kinds of prayer and petitions:

> Finally, be strong in the Lord and in the strength of
> His might. Put on the full armor of God, so that you

will be able to stand firm against the schemes of the devil. For our struggle is not against flesh and blood, but against the rulers, against the powers, against the world forces of this darkness, against the spiritual forces of wickedness in the heavenly places. Therefore, take up the full armor of God, so that you will be able to resist in the evil day, and having done everything, to stand firm. Stand firm therefore, HAVING GIRDED YOUR LOINS WITH TRUTH, and HAVING PUT ON THE BREASTPLATE OF RIGHTEOUSNESS, and having shod YOUR FEET WITH THE PREPARATION OF THE GOSPEL OF PEACE; in addition to all, taking up the shield of faith with which you will be able to extinguish all the flaming arrows of the evil one. And take THE HELMET OF SALVATION, and the sword of the Spirit, which is the word of God.

With all prayer and petition pray at all times in the Spirit, and with this in view, be on the alert with all perseverance and petition for all the saints, and pray on my behalf, that utterance may be given to me in the opening of my mouth, to make known with boldness the mystery of the gospel, for which I am an ambassador in chains; that in proclaiming it I may speak boldly, as I ought to speak. (Ephesians 6:10-18, NASB)

Ruth Graham, wife of Reverend Billy Graham, wrote that she used to pray all night when her rebellious offspring would be doing what she didn't think right, and she would see answers, then the child would do it again, and again. Finally, she told God something like "Just do whatever you want, whatever it takes to bring him to You! That's the goal, and if you have to break both legs, go ahead." (We all know how her children have been leaders in the Christian faith, taking up Billy Graham's work as he aged and passed away!) In the above scripture, it is interesting that the "all prayer and petition" was with the view to give Paul, the writer of Ephesians, words to make known the Christian message! It helped me to read Ruth's words, because as I pray for my grown kids and now grown grand-kids, I do point my prayers in the direction of "whatever it takes" to lead them on in finding and serving our Lord. There is peace in that.

Through all the years of raising the children, Thomas and I prayed together for the children, for the people in our churches, for those in our community who came across our paths with needs, for our leaders, for Jerusalem. We saw many answers to prayer that you would have to say were miraculous, and yet we agonized in prayer over things that seemed immovable. Still, we prayed.

I thank Thomas for showing me so much about prayer; I suppose that is to be expected when you marry a minister. But I also learned that one of my main prayer projects was actually *my husband.* He had tremendous pressure as church leader: imagine a job where you are expected to be brilliant in a new and interesting sermon every week; you have to manage the whole church program and all the committees, always be kind and gentle and caring in every situation, always have answers about any Bible or spiritual question, always be able to counsel anyone in trouble, manage weddings, be the one who has to deliver bad news of death, conduct funerals, spend time with the aging and the very sick, sense who in the congregation wants a visit and who doesn't, etc., etc. And he was always working on the post-graduate degrees—and raising four step-children as though they were his own.

Being the closest person to him, I knew his strengths, and I knew his weaknesses. That is a real privilege, to be that close to a man of God, and God had to help me to see that with that privilege came the responsibility to be a helper, not a *hinderer.* A woman can choose which she wants to be. She can take offense if her husband lets down his guard around her and perhaps blows off steam that would lose him his job if done in public, or she can take it as a compliment that he trusts her so much that he can be realest of real with her, confident that showing that side of what is bugging him will trigger more prayer power from her *for* him, not criticism or judgment. I had to learn that by trial and error, and I admit that sometimes it was more trial and my error.

Just this week, I saw a lovely real life illustration of how I *wish* I had always reacted. Thomas was having a sort of bad day, and was upset at a silly situation with neighbor dogs *again* getting into his own dog's food, dragging the bag of dog food out of the shed and spreading it around. Our grandchildren were here, and I was annoyed that he was using *that tone*. But our tiny grandchild Lily, who adores him, just reached up and took his hand and said, "Poppa, what's wrong?" in the sweetest voice. He melted, of course. Why hadn't I thought of that? If I adore my husband, and I really do even when irritated, then he should feel that I am on his side, against anything that is pressuring him, praying for him to have strength in weaknesses, to have power when he wants to quit, to get a touch from God when he needs it most. We have prayer power when we don't focus on ourselves, but on others. Everything isn't always about us.

> Look not every man on his own things, but every man
> also on the things of others. (Philippians 2:4 KJV)

After watching and learning from Lily, I determined to remember it for the next time hubby used "that tone." It wasn't long. He had a lot of things on his mind. His car was misbehaving (that's *big* for a guy), and our entire property needed weeded and watered, and it was 97 degrees outside. He came in exhausted, thirsty and hungry. I had been working on a painting, and if you can believe it, lost track of the time. When I looked up in surprise, and said, "Oh, lunchtime already?" his look, his words and his tone were exasperated. I felt hurt that he took it out on me, just because I don't have a clock in my head (or a calendar either), and my natural fleshly self wanted to say, "That is just the way I am, so you are insensitive to me to be angry." That would be putting *him* down for me not managing my own weakness, my time mismanagement, and would surely blast a pothole in our path for the day. I required myself to sympathize with his having to work outside in such beastly weather, and then sweetly made him lunch and put a note with it that said, "You are loved." I overlooked his tone and words, and owned up to my own shortcoming. No blame game, just sympathy and going on with what we can do. The path was smoothed out, and we were fine.

> If you've gotten anything at all out of following Christ, if his love has made any difference in your life, if being in a community of the Spirit means anything to you, if you have a heart, if you *care*—then do me a favor: Agree with each other, love each other, be deep-spirited friends. Don't push your way to the front....Put yourself aside, and help others.... Don't be obsessed with getting your own advantage. Forget yourselves long enough to lend a helping hand. (Philippians 2:1-4, MSG)

As heavenly women, we don't need to agonize about whether we know how to pray. Especially with our own children and husband, we know them better than anyone, and we know their weaknesses. Just put your own desires and needs aside and open your heart to the Holy Spirit, and let the prayers flow out of your heart, your unique woman's heart. Women naturally have compassion and sensitivity to others' needs. We are made for this!

LIVING IT

Find a pretty notebook and jot prayers in it, with the date. Leave an empty line below for God's answer. Then leave the prayer with the Lord. When an answer comes, in God's time, put the answer, with the date. You will treasure this in years to come, believe me. I still read over my prayer journals from time to time, and invariably I say, "I can't believe I forgot THAT wonderful answer to prayer! Thank you, Lord!"

FOR FUN

Set a "pray" event on your phone to go off three times a day. We often mean to pray but get busy and forget. I love that my phone can remind me with a little ding and a banner that says "prayer time." These are for quick "arrow prayers" that you can just send off. I usually have one or two current prayers that I feel I am called to be reminding God about, and it just takes a second to turn my heart toward them and God.

Another fun thing to do is to send up little prayers tied to jobs you are doing. When I iron Thomas's shirts, I pray for the dear person who will wear it, and for those he will minister to. When I pick up a little Barbie doll shoe I pray for the tiny grandgirl who left it on the floor. There is an infinite supply of ways to pray for people. You are a secret helper, not only picking up after people and ironing for people, but helping them by your prayers! You are becoming a heavenly woman.

Chapter 11

THE THANKFUL WOMAN
– EUCHARISTEO

Eucharisteo (pronounced yoo-kar-is-*tay*'-oh),
according to the dictionary
is to be grateful, feel thankful, and to give thanks.

Being married to a minister, I was very familiar with the Eucharist, or in layman terms, Holy Communion. I loved the sacrament, loved kneeling at the altar with glowing light filtering through the stained glass windows. I could feel the grace of God and his holy presence as I tasted bread and fruit of the vine, remembering Jesus's last supper and his last words to his disciples before his day of death.

Unfortunately, we didn't have stained glass windows in the parsonage, just regular ones that often needed cleaning. Somehow that beautiful church experience with God seemed far away when it wasn't just God and I by the altar. Back when the kids were all still in the nest, they got hungry every few hours, they got their clothes dirty, they needed help with homework, bean bugs ate the green beans in my garden, my husband had his own burdens to bear plus some papers for me to type, while our neighbor's dog barked endlessly. Sometimes it was hard to be joyful. I wish I had known then what I have discovered now, and maybe I could have brought that stained-glass aura home from church with me.

What were Jesus's last words to us before his ordeal? What were his best and final words to us, knowing he was going to be killed? *Eucharisteo* is what the Greek says: "He gave thanks." Then He said to remember this. *Really? That's it?*

> And when He had taken some bread and given thanks, He broke it and gave it to them, saying, "This is My body which is given for you; do this in remembrance of Me." (Luke 22:19 NASB)

> The Lord Jesus in the night in which He was betrayed took bread; and when He had given thanks, He broke it and said, "This is My body, which is for you; do this in remembrance of Me…as often as you eat this bread and drink the cup. (1 Corinthians 11:23,24, 26 NASB)

Somehow I had always understood it to mean only that "as often as you take communion, remember Christ's death." It does mean that, but I think it also means "give thanks," as often as you eat bread and drink the cup—which is three times a day—and always remember Christ's sacrifice for you. He wants you to always remember how precious you are to him, how deep is His love for you, and that He gave His life for you. He provides our daily bread, and He tells us not to worry, because He has us covered. Not just at church at the Communion rail, but at the dinner table too. The one where hungry kids show up every few hours, and the one that has heaps of dirty pots and pans in the adjoining kitchen waiting to be washed. That's where He wants to be remembered, with a thankful heart! Not just with saying "grace" (eucharisteo), but with our thankful heart and our grateful attitude in the middle of it all.

Just a couple of years ago, our ladies' Bible study group

studied Ann Voskamp's *One Thousand Gifts.* She woke us all up to how giving thanks is central to the Christian message, even as the Eucharist is the central sacrament of all Christianity. She also discovered, and passed along to us, that buried in the center of the word *eucharisteo* is *charis,* which means grace, and *chara,* meaning joy. When we "say grace," what we mean is we are saying thanks, as evidenced by the same sacrament, the Eucharist, in the church sometimes being called The Great Thanksgiving.

Ann brought us up short and caused us to look around us, and see how many gifts we take for granted that are given to us by God. Her own journey challenged us to start a list of gifts from God that we are thankful for, little things that are delightful: songs of a bird sent to serenade us but that we had tuned out; the delicateness of a tiny blue wildflower that we had stomped over as we rushed through life. Things like that. It was incredible to see how many gifts were all around us, and we began to thank God for them as we noticed them. We actually began to be hunters of beauty, hunters of gifts. Life became almost a treasure hunt, and the surprising thing was the sparks of joy we felt as we added things to our list and gave thanks. It appeared that giving thanks was tied somehow to the joy in our hearts.

Jesus "gave thanks," on the eve of his brutal betrayal and impending horrible death, looking forward to the joy that would result:

> fixing our eyes on Jesus, the author and perfecter of faith, who for the joy set before Him endured the cross, despising the shame, and has sat down at the right hand of the throne of God. (Hebrews 12:2 NASB)

And not only that, when we become Christians, we are, when remembering Him in our thanks at Holy Communion, *and at our own tables,* sharing in His death and His resurrection joy:

> Is not the cup of blessing which we bless a sharing
> in the blood of Christ? Is not the bread which we
> break a sharing in the body of Christ? (1 Corinthians
> 10:16, NASB)

It is remarkable too that He talks about just bread and fruit of the vine, two very ordinary supper items, and says, "as often as you eat it," give thanks and remember. That brings it all home to where we don't have stained glass. Our own supper table. Our own laundry room. Our own kitchen. Give thanks to God in all of it, remembering how He gave his only son for us. But here is the amazing part: after we are thankful, *joy* follows.

I am amazed at how many years I walked around blind to the gifts God was giving me. Now, as I seek them out and look for them, even look hard sometimes, I am astounded at His loving gifts. Just hunting for them and counting them brings unexpected joy.

One year a long time ago when money was very tight, I made Christmas presents for the children. Gordon was about six, I think, and he just loved the Curious George children's books. I got the bright idea of making him a Curious George monkey. I found some brown cloth and made a long-legged, long-armed, rather odd-faced monkey, which I thought he would recognize as George. On Christmas morning, when he opened the box, the look on his face was one of stupefaction and bewilderment. He tried to be thankful, but even to this day in his midlife years, he remembers that awful monkey. He now understands the love that went into making it for him, but then it was hard to be thankful. Sometimes things in our lives, like too high a pile of dirty laundry, too many chores, too many demands on our time, make it hard to be thankful. But God, like even me with my needle, has a great love for us and is doing the best for us at the time, even if it is teaching us how to be grateful in hard times.

Sometimes we get an ugly monkey in life. Heavenly women see the loving heart of God behind it and give thanks. Joy comes.

We knew a person who used to have huge birthday parties for his children, inviting all the relatives and friends. It sounds like a great idea to celebrate the birth of a great kid, right? But all it took was for a child to open piles of gifts and then look for more gifts and say, "Is that all?" for his dad to decide to celebrate a little differently.

I wonder at God's infinite patience with me, to wait until I was past middle age to really start getting some thanks, some appreciation for all He does for me and gives me. Now I am cultivating the habit of looking for the special gifts, and life has become so colorful and joyful. One of the ladies in our Bible study group told of how she makes a certain long car trip regularly and it was really boring and tiring, until she opened her eyes and started looking for beauty and gifts along the way, and said it was wonderful.

The opposite of thankful is to be ungrateful. That is an ugly word, and I really am embarrassed to say that I was ungrateful for many years. Not just with God's big gifts, but ordinary things around me. I don't want to take anything for granted anymore, and I am trying to sincerely thank those around me who are kind to me. I thank my husband for the many many things he does around the house and garden, as well as providing for me. I thank my grown kids for their thoughtful deeds and gifts. I thank my grand-kids for coming to visit. I try to let people know their care has not been overlooked.

I recently read a scripture that was very encouraging. Did you know that the very angels of heaven listen to our thanks? Ah, I think we are onto something that will help us along our journey to becoming Heavenly Women!

> Thank you! Everything in me says "Thank you!"
> Angels listen as I sing my thanks.

I kneel in worship facing your holy temple
and say it again: "Thank you!"
Thank you for your love,
thank you for your faithfulness. (Psalm 138:1,2 MSG)

LIVING IT:

Start a list of gifts, God's little encouragements, all around you. Ann Voskamp suggests keeping a simple tablet and pen on our kitchen counter, so we can quickly jot a phrase like, "a beam of sunlight making the wood grain on the floor beautiful." What do you see that delights your soul? Jot it down. Number the list, and be amazed at the number of gifts. Maybe, like Ann, you will list 1000 gifts too!

Look at the many scriptures I found that encourage us to be thankful, on the following page!

FOR FUN:

Send a real snail-mail thank you to someone. Say "thank you" to someone who waits on you. Say "thank you" to a family member. Have fun with "thanks," and enjoy the joy.

EUCHARISTEO—a TREASURE TROVE OF BEING THANKFUL IN THE BIBLE:

Luke 22:19
1 Corinthians 11:23-24
1 Corinthians 10:16
Luke 17:15-16
Psalm 50:23
Matthew 11:25
Philippians 4:11-12
Ephesians 5:20
Luke 1:46
Psalm 69:30
Daniel 6:10
1 Timothy 2:1
1 Thessalonians 5:18
1 Chronicles 16:34
Ezra 3:11
Psalm 7:17
Psalm 9:1
Psalm 69:30
Psalm 95:2
Psalm 100:4
(Almost every Psalm)
Isaiah 51:3
Jeremiah 30:19
Daniel 6:10
Matthew 14:19
Matthew 26:26
Mark 8:6-7
Mark 14:22-23

John 6:23
Acts 27:35
Romans 1:21
Romans 6:17
2 Corinthians 4:15
2 Corinthians 9:11-15
Ephesians 5:4
Philippians 4:6
Colossians 3:17
1 Thessalonians 5:18
1 Timothy 4:4
Revelation 11:17
Matthew 26:26
Mark 8:6-7
Mark 14:22-23
John 6:23
Acts 27:35
Romans 1:21
Romans 6:17
2 Corinthians 4:15
2 Corinthians 9:11-15
Ephesians 5:4
Philippians 4:6
Colossians 3:17
1 Thessalonians 5:18
1 Timothy 4:4
Revelation 11:17

Chapter 12

THE LOVING WOMAN—
ALL KINDS OF LOVE

We women have all dreamed of finding Prince Charming from the time we first heard the fairy tales; then some time in our teens or early adulthood we get hit by cupid's arrow, and "fall in love." The Greek word used in the New Testament for romantic, sensual love is *eros*. It is heady, breathtaking, and all-consuming. Probably God gave it to us as part of his plan to get us married and settled down and starting a family; but sometime, perhaps years after the honeymoon is over, or in the middle of a huge disagreement with our mate, we can wonder where the love is. Part of the problem is that we don't understand that *eros* is not the only kind of love God puts in our natures.

A mother's love for her child is a different kind of love completely—the world celebrates it, honors it, puts it on a pedestal. This is the Greek *storge* word for love that the Greeks used when describing natural family love, and it is the love we women feel not only for our babies but for our mate. Our love towards our husbands, while still being *eros* love, expands to also include a familiar, comfortable, trusting love that makes a home a sanctuary from the outside world. It is a place where we know and accept each other's strengths and weaknesses without judgment. It is a place where we know what each likes and doesn't like, as nobody else does outside the family home. It is a long-term, belonging type of love.

Speaking of mother-love, one of my older sisters had twin boys, and their names were James and John. I don't know if she knew when she named them that in the Bible James and John were called "the sons of thunder," but it sure turned out that way for her twins. They were double trouble, but they were really cute and very smart little guys, even actually wiring their tree house with electricity when they were just little kids. As they became teenagers, they started having friends who were a bit wild, and they themselves struggled. They were in such constant conflict with parents that even I, their aunt, was worn out from praying for them. But not their mom. She prayed and prayed for them and always believed in them. She never gave up on them. They were in and out of marriages and relationships, and in and out of difficulties. It wasn't until they were middle aged that both began to go to church and served God, but all through their young years she never doubted that they would turn to God some time. I remember thinking, "Only a mother can love like that!" That's *storge* love!

It is amazing the love that a mother has for her little ones. *Storge* love is a love that even mother animals have for their litters. It has nothing to do with how good a person the mother is, but rests more on how cute the little one is. (It may break down when the little one ceases to be cute or sweet, which is where teenage troubles come in.)

The mother is the one who holds the keys to a child's heart. She has the power to keep the children or drive them away. She is the one who loves the child more than anyone else on earth, yet sometimes she doesn't know how to convey that to the child. She can become a real nag to the child, without really giving loving direction—then the child does not feel the bond he or she needs to grow up, to mature, and to spread wings successfully. A wise woman disciplines the child, but only in love. She teaches the children the way to go, but is always trying to let them know she is holding their hearts. Look at Proverbs 23:12-16:

> Apply your heart to discipline
> And your ears to words of knowledge.
> Do not hold back discipline from the child,
> Although you strike him with
> the rod, he will not die.
> You shall strike him with the rod
> And rescue his soul from Hell.
> My son, if your heart is wise,
> My own heart also will be glad;
> And my inmost being will rejoice
> When your lips speak what is right.
> Do not let your heart envy sinners, But
> live in the fear of the Lord always.
> Surely there is a future, And your
> hope will not be cut off.
> Listen, my son, and be wise, And
> direct your heart in the way.
> Do not be with heavy drinkers of wine,
> Or with gluttonous eaters of meat;
> For the heavy drinker and the glutton will come to
> poverty, And drowsiness will clothe one with rags.
> Listen to your father who begot you,
> And do not despise your mother when she is old.
> Buy truth, and do not sell it,
> *Get* wisdom and instruction and understanding.
> The father of the righteous will greatly rejoice,
> And he who sires a wise son will be glad in him.
> Let your father and your mother be glad,
> And let her rejoice who gave birth to you.
> Give me your heart, my son,
> And let your eyes delight in my ways. (Proverbs
> 23:12—26, NASB)

Scan through the passage above and see how many times you can find the word "heart." If there were only one chapter in the Old Testament that a mother could have to reach her children, this would be it. Read the entire chapter to see the scope of what the parent is teaching the children! I call it the "heart chapter."

Above all, capture the heart of your child while they are little, and they will be bound to you forever in love. Hold the child in your heart. Look at verse 26, "Give me your heart, my son." I knew a woman who amazed me at how she kept her children in her heart. They obeyed her immediately and lovingly, because they couldn't bear to damage the love bond they felt with her. Even when she had to discipline them, she managed to show them that she hated doing it, but because she loved them so, and because she loved God who commanded her to discipline them, she *had* to do it. She never got into the name-calling and yelling that we hear in the world around us so often. She inspired me (and often made me feel very inadequate—but that's why we have people we look up to).

I wish I had shown more love to my little ones when I disciplined them, but we all do what we think is best with the knowledge and experience we have at the time. When my chicks were finally grown, and our era of discipline was finished, they flew from our nest—but not always in a direction we had pointed out to them. But never, ever did it affect the love I felt for them. If they needed us, Thomas and I would be there for them, and they knew it. It doesn't mean that we couldn't remind them if we felt their flight path was headed for the rocks, but we had to let them be free human beings. The nest time was over, but they were welcome any time to visit the nest and enjoy the feeling of being a loved part of the family. And they always knew we would pray for them; if something bad happened in their lives, they would call and ask us to pray.

The sons-in-law and daughters-in-law, too, have always been welcome. Sometimes it takes a pro-active effort to make them feel welcome, but that is important. Our mother-love will extend into grandmother-love in time, so a wise mother-in-law will keep that in mind from the beginning. I always told my daughters-in-law and son-in-law that they could complain all they wanted to me about their mates, because I'm a safe one to unload on. Think about it: if they unload to their own mothers, their own mothers may dislike or resent the spouse because they have no natural bond. I, on the other hand, will never love my kids less no matter what bad I hear about them, and I can sympathize with the in-law and pray for my progeny as nobody else can.

Recent brain research made possible with the advance in MRI imaging has brought some interesting facts that a wise mother will take into account. First, the pathways in the brain are "pruned" in adolescence, where the old pathways of childhood start to dissolve and the ones needed to become independent and mature are strengthened. You may look at the surly expression on your teenager's face and say inside, "that is the same face I used to pat and kiss as I rocked him, back when I was the most important person in his life—who *is* this person?" Relax, their brains are maturing, leaving childhood behind; rejoice that they are on their way to maturity. Remind yourself that they are just "on their way," not there yet. Their brains are not finished yet, so don't expect more than they are capable of. Second, the part of the brain that experiences emotion grows faster in adolescence than the part that uses reason or logic, so even though you think you can reason with them, you often find their reaction is just emotional, reactionary. It's ok. Third, the part of the brain that processes risk gets lopsided during adolescence, where even though they know some things are risky, their brain downplays the negative consequences and amplifies the upside of risk. I, for one, remember my teen and early adult years when risky behavior or daring activities were very attractive, but now that my brain is older, I feel more content to choose a safer thing. Heavenly women can remind themselves when their kids are going through brain metamorphosis that it isn't permanent; they will also mature in time and choose better paths. Wait and pray. Watching my older sister who waited patiently for her sons of thunder to mature (which they did, as they became wonderful Christian adults!) helped me to try to do the same for my teens and young adults.

> Older women likewise are to be reverent in their behavior, not malicious gossips nor enslaved to much wine, teaching what is good, so that they may encourage the young women to love their husbands, to love their children, to be sensible, pure, workers at home, kind, being subject to their own husbands, so that the word of God will not be dishonored. (Titus 2:3—5, NASB)

Actually, the Greek word used in the scripture we read in Titus that encourages the older women to teach the younger women to "love their husbands" and to "love their children" is another kind of love, *phileo*: to be fond of, to build a friendship with, to prefer the company of them. This can be viewed as the "fun" part of being a wife and parent. The heavenly woman will either get creative on her own, if she is that type of creative person, or she can learn to use others' ideas, but this scripture tells the woman to see to this.

There are lots of ways to build a friendship with your husband. The *eros* part of the relationship, especially when we are young, pretty much takes care of itself naturally, but it takes a little work to keep the *phileo* friendship thing going. Take time to ask him his opinion of things, what he thinks of the news or situations. Time is important here: give him your undivided attention as you visit over things. Beware of trying to catch up on your many things you have to do while listening to him. While women are naturally able to multi-task, men are more focused on one thing, and he will feel like he is being sandwiched in among other things if you try to do other things like handwork or housework while he is talking to you. Take time for him. Look into his eyes as he talks—eye contact helps you see into his soul, and helps him see someone who is focused on him. Also, in addition to listening time, be creative about doing some fun things and building memories together.

When my children were growing up, I was always on the lookout for books with ideas about fun ways to celebrate holidays, ideas for rainy days, or ideas for vacations. As the kids grow into adults, you can still do this to keep fun and friendship in the relationship. Actually, when the child is an adult, you are finally free to be their friend without telling them what to do! If you respect him or her as another adult, and don't put pressure to do things or live life the way you want, you will enjoy the friendship. If you have trained them up the way they should go, you don't have to harp on that, or dwell on it. Build the love and fellowship up, and pray blessings on them. Be a safe and comforting place for them if they need it.

Phileo love is also the kind of love we show towards friends. It includes fun and fellowship, when things are going well, but it can break down if someone gets offended. Church splits and fusses happen when phileo fails.

Don't feel guilty if you have had a breakdown in your relationships with your husband, your friends, your children or grandchildren. Actually, the *storge* love we feel for that darling baby that comes into our lives is doomed to fail at some point. Also the *phileo* love that we work so hard to cultivate in both our family and our friend circle will have some ups and downs too as our interests and values change, and we can run out of steam to even be friends with our children, especially teenagers. It isn't that the *storge* or *phileo* loves are bad, it is just that they sooner or later are not enough. They are natural, human instincts, and, well, we are human. So instead of feeling like we are failures, we should realize that we just have not been taught that there is another way.

> And I show you a still more excellent way. (1 Corinthians 12:31b, NASB)

> Love is patient, love is kind and is not jealous; love does not brag and is not arrogant, does not act unbecomingly; it does not seek its own, is not provoked, does not take into account a wrong suffered, does not rejoice in unrighteousness, but rejoices with the truth; bears all things, believes all things, hopes all things, endures all things. Love never fails. (1 Corinthians 13:4—8, NASB)

The Greek word for love in the above verses is *agape*. Agape means God's kind of love and goodwill. Our natural loves, *eros* for our husband, the *storge* and *phileo* family-love, mother-love and friend-love are all almost the opposite of *agape,* God's kind of love. Where verse 4 says *"agape* is patient," you can tell yourself, *"eros, storge* or *phileo* can be impatient." Where it says *"agape* is kind," we can say that *"eros, storge* or *phileo* can be unkind,"* etc. Thankfully, verse 8 says, *"agape* love never fails."

But how do we get this amazing God-kind-of-love, *agape* love? When our own natural (*eros, storge* or *phileo*) love has failed us, what should we do? We read on to the next verse:

> Pursue [agape] love, yet desire earnestly spiritual *gifts.* (1 Corinthians 14:1 NASB)

The word "pursue," according to the dictionary, is to follow someone or something in order to catch it! So this agape love may seem far ahead of us, out of our grasp, but we run after it as best we can. But the Apostle Paul goes on to say help has arrived: "desire earnestly spiritual gifts." What we hope for will happen, and will not disappoint! Agape love is one of the fruits, or results, of the Holy Spirit of God promised in Galatians 5:22, so when we ask God to fill us with his Holy Spirit, God Himself pours *agape* love into our hearts!

> ...and hope does not disappoint, because the [agape] love of God has been poured out within our hearts through the Holy Spirit who was given to us. (Romans 5:5, NASB)

Agape love is an action, not a feeling. *Agape* love is the love that we can "put on" just as we would put on an article of clothing. (This is not the same "put on" as describing something fake!) We can actually turn our focus inward to our own souls and say, "I know I don't feel like loving this person right now; but I am going to do loving things and speak loving words. I am going to do this as God gives me the strength to do so." And we ask God, right then and there, to fill us again with this *agape* love, to "pour out within our hearts" this God-kind of love.

> Put on [agape] love, the bond of unity (Colossians 3:14 NASB)

Even though we now understand that the teen and even early 20's brain is not functioning as a mature adult yet, we still struggle with their ill tempers, depression, and sulkiness. We also know our mates are not angelic beings, nor are we (yet), and there are times when we just don't feel the *eros*. Our *storge* and *phileo* instinctive loves just aren't enough. When we feel that frustration and inability to respond kindly, remember:

> I can do all things through Christ, who strengthens me. (Philippians 4:13, NASB)

How exactly do we "do all things through Christ"? By asking Him to fill us with His Spirit! Here is a prayer you can pray when you are at your wits' end about your children:

> "Lord, this child (or grown son or daughter) is one that you have given me to raise for you, and in many ways I have failed to follow your instructions, so we have some trouble. I now dedicate the child (or grown son or daughter) to you, and ask you, in your grace, to forgive my errors and to make it up to them some way. I leave him/her in your hands. Please fill me with your Holy Spirit so that I may have your *agape* love for them, and I pray that this love will help me to be firmly planted in my child's heart over time."

And here is a prayer for our mate when things seem to be going badly:

> "Lord, this man who you have given to me to love and cherish and comfort is hard to understand, and sometimes we have failed to follow your directions for our roles in our home, so we have trouble. I commit to being a heavenly woman in every way that I can, as you give me the strength. Please fill me with your Holy Spirit and pour your love into my heart, as you have promised. I pray that this agape love will help me to be firmly planted in his heart."

LIVING IT:

Make a point of BEING loving, no matter how your natural feelings are toward your mate or children. (This works even if you don't think they are living up to your ideals.) Try to sort out whether you are trying to just love out of the natural instincts of eros, phileo, or storge loves, or whether you are relying on God to supply the heavenly agape love by His Holy Spirit.

FOR FUN:

Take time for your mate, a friend, or your family. Take time to listen and look at them as they talk. Try to hear their heart. Think of some fun activity to do with them—especially something *they* would think is fun.

Chapter 13

THE KIND WOMAN—
OVERLOOKING OTHERS' FAULTS

Truly great accessorizing: Colossians 3:12,
"Put on a heart of...kindness..."

When I was doing "color analysis" professionally years ago,
I would determine which style type a person was, and help
them learn what looked good on them and what was awful for
them. God's infinite variety of humans, although each unique,
can be sort of divided into general types, ranging from tall and
dramatic to earthy and natural to classic perfection to sporty and
bouncy to dainty and petite, and everything in between. People
were amazed to find their own style type, and a list of their
best and their worst clothing styles, accessories, hairstyles and
makeup looks. Many of my clients had been wearing things that
were unbecoming to them, not knowing that just making some
different choices could alter how they felt about themselves, and
how people perceived them. After their "makeover," they knew
how to avoid the negatives of their type and how to accentuate
the positives.

I remember one woman who was tall and bony, with rather
irregular features, who had retreated to wearing just jeans and

t-shirts for years because "cute" or "pretty" clothes felt all wrong. I showed her that she was the "dramatic" type, which looks good in bold colors and unusual designs, not frills or daintiness. She came out of the shadows, so to speak, and gave herself permission to try clothing and accessories that were bright and exciting, not frilly or cutesy. Her complexion was olive, dark hair and eyes, and she had tried using pink lipstick and blush, but it wasn't flattering, so she stopped wearing makeup. I showed her how her coloring was accented perfectly by deep, sheer cranberry lip and cheek color. She was stunning, to her own surprise, as well as to those in her life. Suddenly she looked like a striking model. (Think of Cher's style and coloring!)

Another woman had considered herself so average that she felt boring. Her height and build were medium, her hair medium ash brown and her eyes a medium blue-gray. She had given up on makeup and fashion, thinking that whole thing belonged to the dramatic model types. Imagine her amazement and delight to find out that she was the "classic" type, who could wear the simple, sophisticated Chanel suit style elegantly. Her light coloring was framed beautifully in soft blue-gray or heather-green clothing, and dusty-rose blush and lips rounded out her beautiful, graceful and tasteful look. (Think Princess Grace, or Kate Middleton!)

Another client was an avid horsewoman, with a sturdy frame and natural features. She had given up on trying to be pretty, simply declaring, "I'm natural." She was right about her style type, but surprised to find a variety of fabrics, styles and colors that transforms the "natural" woman. I showed her that her eyes were not just brown, but shades of cinnamon, gold, and green. A touch of brown eye shadow to accent her great eyes, a little cinnamon blush and lipstick, a rust-colored shirt—and viola! She was gorgeous. (Imagine Julia Roberts or Raquel Welch!)

For these women, all it took was finding their type, embracing the "good" and avoiding the "bad" lists, and then enjoying their own unique gifts from God. What we did in my studio was fun, even life-changing, but dealt with appearance and surface things, not the inner person. This is an outer word picture of a deeper parallel of discovering the personality type of the inner person.

Thomas used a similar approach in his Christian counseling sessions, helping people find their personality type and then learn to minimize their negatives and accentuate their positives. Each personality type has a list of both, and just learning where we fit into the spectrum can be a real eye-opener. It can be like a beauty makeover for the inner person! We can learn to be on the lookout for when we, in our natural tendencies, are about to operate in the negative list, and we can look for ways to live in the best parts of our personality type. That is a learned behavior, and it is something we can use to improve ourselves. All those around us have their own personality types too, and once we learn about personality types, we can understand better "why" they do and say what they do and say. Understanding them makes it easier to be *kind* and not judgmental of them when they do and say things very differently than we do and say them.

I remember one particular story at a church where Thomas was the minister that illustrated the personality types so well. Thomas is a very classic type, and he likes order, neatness, and regularity. The choir director was very different, liking spontaneity, serendipity, and last-minute changes. You can imagine that there was some friction, and week by week it seemed to get worse, until it looked like they could not work together any longer. Then one Sunday Thomas happened to share in a sermon about the different personality types, and how although humans come in a huge variety of personalities, they can be divided into the four categories, which he described. A light came on for the choir director, and he said afterward, "Oh! I see why we have not gotten along—we are just opposite personality types! You are the type who lines up his shoes neatly, and I half the time can't even find my shoes!" After that, he made allowances for their different approaches instead of thinking, "What is wrong with the pastor that he doesn't think and do the way I think and do?" They learned to work together.

Once we realize that the person who really irritates us is just operating out of their own type and style, we shouldn't take it personally. We can give them the opportunity to pick between their personality type's "good" and "bad" list, and not be too hard on them when they make wrong choices. We can be *kind* to them, as we hope others are kind to us when we fall short.

> Be kindly affectioned one to another with brotherly love; in honour preferring one another; (Romans 12:10 KJV)

The last chapter explored the two words that make up the Greek word for "kindly affectioned", which are phileo and storge, signifying friendship and family love. Therefore, it means "cherishing, being fond of parents, children and fellow humans." Some versions say, "putting on a heart of kindness." People think that the "falling in love," passionate *eros* love you have toward your mate, is what married love is, but there is also this warm, human, comfortable and welcoming love. This loving kindness is what carries you through rough spots when you are going through life together, as friends, as family. This is the love that undergirds and supports your eros love. Eros, the flaming love God designed between a man and a woman, can cool over time if there is not the *phileo-storge* kind of love growing beneath it to support it in its faltering times.

Here we want to look at the importance of a woman "putting on a heart of kindness." Our Christian beauty makeover would not be complete without accessories. *Not the putting on of pearls,* but the putting on of *kindness.*

> So, chosen by God for this new life of love, dress in the wardrobe God picked out for you: compassion, kindness, humility, quiet strength, discipline.

Be even-tempered, content with second place,
quick to forgive an offense. Forgive as quickly
and completely as the Master forgave you. And
regardless of what else you put on, wear love. It's
your basic, all-purpose garment. Never be without
it. (Colossians 3:12—14 the Message)

We want to be heavenly women, but we need to have the
help of the Holy Spirit. In our own strength, we will end up in
our negative list on the days when we don't have the intestinal
fortitude to be all we should be. We don't always feel like being
kind when that other person is acting from their negative list.
It is easy to forget that when others fail to be their best self, we
can still be *kind* and overlook their failure. As someone chosen
by God (that's you, or you wouldn't be in this study!), you have
a mission and a calling right where you are, right in the middle
of human beings who are different types, who fail, who need
your kindness.

Those of us who are strong and able in the faith
need to step in and lend a hand to those who falter,
and not just do what is most convenient for us.
Strength is for service, not status. Each one of us
needs to look after the good of the people around
us, asking ourselves, "How can I help?"

That's exactly what Jesus did. He didn't make it easy
for himself by avoiding people's troubles, but waded
right in and helped out. "I took on the troubles of
the troubled," is the way Scripture puts it. Even if
it was written in Scripture long ago, you can be
sure it's written for us. God wants the combination
of his steady, constant calling and warm, personal
counsel in Scripture to come to characterize us,
keeping us alert for whatever he will do next. May
our dependably steady and warmly personal God
develop maturity in you so that you get along with

> each other as well as Jesus gets along with us all.
> Then we'll be a choir—not our voices only, but our
> very lives singing in harmony in a stunning anthem
> to the God and Father of our Master Jesus! (Romans
> 15:1-6 The Message (MSG)

Being kind to others, especially our mate, when we don't feel he deserves it, can be hard. How can we get this endurance and strength? There is a secret that we can write in our minds and hearts that will help us with being kind to parents, children, mates, fellow humans, when they act unkind towards us or otherwise don't "deserve" our kindness. I have said it many times, and repeat it again: ask the Holy Spirit to fill us. Pray for *myself* to be *kind.* Pray for the other that they will grow strong in their choice between their good list and their bad list. After all, we ourselves have to choose every day, every hour, which list we will follow. Some days, we do better than others, but we still want to be loved and forgiven. We want others to overlook our shortcomings. The great Golden Rule works both ways:

> Here is a simple, rule-of-thumb guide for behavior:
> Ask yourself what you want people to do for you,
> then grab the initiative and do it for them. Add up
> God's Law and Prophets and this is what you get.
> (Matthew 7:12 MSG)

There is a Hebrew word used in the Old Testament for *kindness,* which gives us another facet of meaning. When you look at words as though they were diamonds with many facets, you can find more ways to "get hold of them" and use them. The Hebrew word is "chen" (pronounced khane), meaning "gracious, kind, well favored, precious, and pleasant." I like the last facet, "pleasant." Pleasant and kind go hand in hand. "Kind," in the dictionary is: humane, benevolent, good-hearted, sympathetic, generous, friendly. Pleasant is: agreeable, acceptable, affable, good, friendly, obliging, grateful, gratifying, cheerful. Which of these adjectives do you think that your mate and family would use in describing you? Which of the adjectives would you *like* to *add* to your beauty kit? When you are irritated with others, it is a great time to pray for yourself that you will be full of *kindness* and *kind thoughts*. These come from the Holy Spirit. Love, joy, peace, patience, kindness, goodness, faithfulness, gentleness, and self-control—Galatians 5:22,23—all these are fruits of the Spirit.

There is an ancient beauty secret to help you add the traits of kindness to your own personality. Above, we read Galatians 5:22-23 in the traditional New American version, but see if it helps to read it in The Message version:

> But what happens when we live God's way [being filled with the Spirit]? He brings gifts into our lives, much the same way that fruit appears in an orchard—things like affection for others, exuberance about life, serenity. We develop a willingness to stick with things, a sense of compassion in the heart, and a conviction that a basic holiness permeates things and people. We find ourselves involved in loyal commitments, not needing to force our way in life, able to marshal and direct our energies wisely. (Galatians 5:22,23 MSG)

Being filled with the Holy Spirit will not change your personality type--you will always be a dynamic outgoing leader, or a quiet follower, or whatever your particular type is—but *kindness* will be ADDED as jewelry to an outfit. Every personality type is enhanced by adding the facets of kindness and pleasantness.

There are four major personality categories, and we are often a blend of two or more types. Jesus is the perfect blend of all four, and the closer we come to Him and the more we are controlled by the Holy Spirit, the more balanced we will be. The four types are:

- Choleric (The good list: decisive leader, dynamic, visionary, go-getter. The bad list: volcanic, demanding, bossy, impatient, insensitive, wordy)
- Melancholic (The good list: quiet, introspective, thoughtful, poetic, creative, sensitive. The bad list: isolated, overly sensitive, complaining, may give in to depression, looks on the negative side)
- Phlegmatic (The good list: slow to react, stable, solid, hard worker, dependable, quiet, good follower. The bad list: stubborn, slow to act, holds grudge, withdraws, prefers to not communicate)
- Sanguine (The good list: fun, interested to see how things will turn out, believes the best, outgoing, happy, not introspective, interesting story-teller, creative, leader type who can sell ice to someone in the Arctic, good neighbor. The bad list: shallow, changeable, undependable, often exaggerates, deceptive, selfish, vain).

A fun way to remember the four personality types is to look at four of the memorable women in the Bible who could each demonstrate a personality type:

For a choleric example, we just have to look at Deborah, the only female leader of Israel in the Old Testament. The Israelites had "done evil in the sight of the Lord" and He had let them be captured. When they cried out to God for deliverance, He appointed Deborah, a married woman, to lead them. That was unheard of at the time! She was very wise and was recognized as their "judge," holding court under her own palm tree at her home. Barak, the army leader, was so convinced that God was with Deborah that he insisted that she even go into battle with the army to bring God on the scene! Deborah was a good wife and was called the "mother of Israel," being someone who was good at making decisions and good at hearing from God. But as a choleric woman, she also could be insensitive and unsympathetic. She chided Barak as though he were weak and was condescending.

> And Deborah, a prophetess, the wife of Lapidoth, she judged Israel at that time.
>
> And she dwelt under the palm tree of Deborah between Ramah and Bethel in mount Ephraim: and the children of Israel came up to her for judgment. (Judges 4:4,5 KJV)
>
> And Barak said unto her, If thou wilt go with me, then I will go: but if thou wilt not go with me, then I will not go. And she said, I will surely go with thee: notwithstanding the journey that thou takest shall not be for thine honour; for the LORD shall sell Sisera into the hand of a woman. And Deborah arose, and went with Barak to Kedesh. (Judges 4:8,9 KJV)

To see a melancholic type, we can look at Miriam, the sister of Moses and Aaron. As a small girl she tenderly cared for her baby brother Moses, as she quietly watched over him in the bulrushes, and was clever enough when the Egyptian princess found Moses to pipe up, "Shall I run and find a Hebrew woman to nurse him for you?" Then she quickly fetched her mother, who then was able to nurse and raise Moses until he was old enough to move to the palace and become Prince of Egypt. When Moses and Aaron led the Israelites out of captivity with God's miraculous help through the Red Sea, melancholic Miriam wrote and sang a beautiful song of deliverance that would inspire and encourage the frightened crowd of refugees, and the whole song is recorded for us in the Bible. Some consider it one of the finest song lyrics ever written. However, shortly after that, she became jealous of Moses' leadership position, and found fault with his wives, to the point of spreading dissension among the people. God was angry with her and taught her a lesson that humbled her.

She was sorry, but her former glory never returned, and both she and Moses died before they could enter the Promised Land. It is very important to pay attention to the "good list" and "bad list" for every type; what we were put on the earth to do can be great as we follow God closely, and can be devastating if we succumb to our negative list.

A great example of the phlegmatic type is Ruth. Remember the Bible story of how Ruth, a foreigner, became widowed and followed her Jewish mother-in-law, Naomi, back to Israel? Her dependable devotion and patient care for Naomi is such a beautiful picture of love that it has been incorporated into wedding ceremonies over the centuries, "til death do us part":

> And Ruth said, Entreat me not to leave thee, or to return from following after thee: for whither thou goest, I will go; and where thou lodgest, I will lodge: thy people shall be my people, and thy God my God:

> Where thou diest, will I die, and there will I be buried: the LORD do so to me, and more also, if ought but death part thee and me. (Ruth 1:16,17 KJV)

Phlegmatic Ruth gave up her own culture and home to care for her mother-in-law in a strange land. They were poor, but Ruth went every day and toiled under the hot middle-eastern sun to gather any grain left behind by reapers. By the way, Naomi was very despondent and bitter over losing both her sons, and even told Ruth to quit calling her Naomi, but instead call her "Mara," meaning "bitter." Talk about patience, Ruth was a sure picture of the phlegmatic type, able to just keep on doing what she had to do, not turning left or right, and not turning back. She didn't say much when Naomi peppered her with questions about where she worked or what she did—she said one sentence: "I worked in the field of a rich man named Boaz." Naomi realized that God was working, for Boaz was a distant relative, and she gave

Ruth careful instructions about what to do. All Ruth said was that she would do whatever Naomi told her to do. Boaz noticed her, came over and ate lunch with her, and it wasn't long until they wound up married. Ruth became the great grandmother of King David! The Bible doesn't let us in on any bad days where Ruth might have been in her "bad list" but we really remember her for her "good list."

Observe the Blessed Mary, Mother of Jesus, to understand the Sanguine. She was "in God's eyes beautiful inside and out," according to the angel Gabriel, who came to visit Mary when she was about 14, and still a virgin. She was thrilled when he told her she would bear the Son of God who would be savior of the world, and although at first she said, "But how? I've never slept with a man!" she willingly believed whatever he said! And when he told her about her barren cousin Elizabeth, who was also now miraculously pregnant, she immediately packed up and traveled to see her. The sanguine type quickly believes and quickly acts. When she arrived at Elizabeth's house, she spoke with beauty and joy the speech which has been called the Magnificat. Some of the most interesting and gifted preachers are sanguine, as they have a real way with words. She was aware of the promises in the Sacred Writings about the Messiah, and the last line of her speech shows that she was prophesying that Israel's promises would be fulfilled in her son.

> And Mary said,
> I'm bursting with God-news;
>   I'm dancing the song of my Savior God.
> God took one good look at me, and look what happened—
>   I'm the most fortunate woman on earth!
> What God has done for me will never be forgotten,
>   the God whose very name is holy, set apart from all others.

His mercy flows in wave after wave
    on those who are in awe before him.
He bared his arm and showed his strength,
    scattered the bluffing braggarts.
He knocked tyrants off their high horses,
    pulled victims out of the mud.
The starving poor sat down to a banquet;
    the callous rich were left out in the cold.
He embraced his chosen child, Israel;
    he remembered and piled on the mercies, piled
    them high.
It's exactly what he promised,
    beginning with Abraham and right up to now.
    (Luke 1:16—55, The Message MSG)

When Mary was 9 months pregnant, the government required that she and Joseph make a long journey to be taxed. My husband, who is a choleric type and knows it well, says that if Mary were choleric, instead of sweetly riding a donkey over rough roads for days, she would have said, "This is impossible. How much further is it? Did you remember to make reservations?" If she were phlegmatic, she might have felt a grudge toward the government but held it inside and never said a word. And, if she were melancholic, she might have wept and complained. Perhaps after several rough days she might have joined Job's wife in saying, "Why don't you just curse God and die?" But Mary was Sanguine, believing God was at work, interested to see what would happen next, hospitable to visits by shepherds and sheep in her birthing room, blessing God in the midst of it all. She remembered all the promises that were to be fulfilled through her son. Years later she was in the midst of the riots that led to the murder of her son, still believing God would do what He said, and she was still believing, in the midst of the disciples who gathered on the day of Pentecost to wait on the Holy Spirit to come. The Bible says the Holy Spirit fell on each of them, so her faith was rewarded at last with the Baptism of the Holy Spirit, the completion of the visitation by the Holy Spirit she experienced when she conceived the Son of God.

> Now the birth of Jesus Christ was on this wise: When as his mother Mary was espoused to Joseph, before they came together, she was found with child of the Holy Ghost. (Matthew 1:18 KJV)

> Now there stood by the cross of Jesus his mother, and his mother's sister, Mary the wife of Cleophas, and Mary Magdalene. (John 19:25 KJV)

> These all continued with one accord in prayer and supplication, with the women, and Mary the mother of Jesus, and with his brethren. (Acts 1:14 KJV)

Although I used Mary as an illustration of the sanguine type, and she is fantastic, it doesn't mean sanguine is any better *type* than the other three. *Each personality type is good. Each is designed by God.* Each has its pitfalls to watch out for. We can be the best we can be, as we ask to be filled with the Holy Spirit, who will add love, joy, peace, patience, kindness, goodness, faithfulness, gentleness, and self-control to our natural personalities.

When we find ourselves having to live or work with someone who is very different from ourselves in temperament, and we are impatient with them when they react or don't react the way we think they should, we need to remember that God forgives *us* and helps *us* to change from natural reactions, and He is just as interested in helping *others*. But that is His job, on His timetable. Just as Jesus is kind to us when we falter or when we slip into our "bad list," we should be kind to others when they do. Maybe they don't know God yet, or haven't even heard that there is a Holy Spirit.

> Wherefore receive ye one another, as Christ also
> received us to the glory of God. (Romans 15:7 KJV)

Anita Bryant, Miss Oklahoma and runner-up to Miss America "way back when" (when I was young), is a beautiful woman and a talented singer with many hit songs. But she wrote in her book that she had a problem with kindness. She tells of the time she was doing a concert in Houston. She decided to turn the two-day stay into a sort of mini-honeymoon and packed a brand new pretty nightie. However, their flight was late, travel arrangements got all mixed up, meals were unsatisfactory, etc., etc., and Anita was fussy about it all, and complained and harassed her husband. After her concert was over and she and her husband were back at the hotel room, she got all fixed up and perfumed for a "late night show." She said her husband ignored her and turned over and went to sleep. She was furious. The next day they talked through it, and when she asked him what would have "turned him on," he replied, quietly and sternly, "Kindness, Anita." Anita writes that God revealed to her that day that no matter how pretty you are or how great the outfit, it is only part of the picture. Her "attitude had to match the outfit." We all try to have our accessories match our outfits, but this is the real accessory that matches all outfits, and complements them perfectly: *kindness.*

LIVING IT:

Look at those around you, in your home, your workplace, your school, your church, and see if you can see the various personality types. Rejoice in the variety of God's handiwork, and learn to accept each as their own gift to the world. Be kind to those who are not handling their negative lists well.

Be kind, not judgmental, to those who are of a different personality type. Look for the good traits of that type and not the negative traits; realize that we all have our own lists of good and negative traits and hopefully we all learn to live in the good list.

FOR FUN:

Prayerfully read through the following pages about the four personality types, both the strengths and weaknesses, and see if you can determine your primary personality type. You are a unique individual, and not all items on each type list will apply to you, and you might be primarily one type with some of another type. (You might want to ask your mate or a friend to help you be objective about yourself!) Start two lists of your unique good and negative personality traits as you notice them. Rejoice in the good list! Write down instances of when you acted from either list, as you learn to stay out of the negative list!

The Choleric

(The Good List and Bad List)

Strengths of a Choleric

Practical
Quick thinker
Good trouble shooters
Enthusiastic
Will not give up
Great ambition
Fearless and courageous
Passion to win
Thrilled with opposition
Yearns for great things
Intelligent
Does not complain
Born leader
Strong willed

Weaknesses of a Choleric

Demanding
Domineering
Easily bored
Easily annoyed
Impatient
Bossy and arrogant
Quick tempered
Can't relax
Too impetuous
Inflexible
Is not complimentary
Unsympathetic
Dislikes emotions
Little tolerance for mistakes

Not easily discouraged	Can be rude or tactless
Independent	Sarcastic
Exudes confidence	Critical
Delegates work well	Must be in control
Makes the goal	Has inflated ego
Stimulates others	Holds a grudge
Excels in emergencies	Revengeful
Visionary	Their plan is always "the best"
Likes pressure	Tends to use people
Self-reliant	Decides for others
Energetic	Can do everything "better"
Daring, risk taker	Can't say "I'm sorry"
Decisive	Too independent
Determined	Too busy for family
Doer	May make rash decisions
Direct	Tends to over dominate
Wants results	Enjoys controversy, arguments
Likes to achieve	"Knows everything"
Goal-oriented	Impatient with those who drift

Phlegmatic

(The Good List and the Bad List)

Strengths of a Phlegmatic	Weaknesses of a Phlegmatic
Steady, not moved easily	Introvert
Patient	Watcher, not doer
Free from stress, tend not to worry	Meets requirements, then stops
Lives balanced life	Must be re-started after project
Meek, most gentle people on planet	Unenthusiastic
In control of themselves	Can be very stubborn
In control of their environment	Not team players
Comfortable with themselves	Lazy, gets tired easily
Stays focused on project, gets it done	Struggles with motivating themselves
Dry sense of humor	Tormented by fear
Very witty	Indecisive about the next step
Dependable	Avoids responsibilities, extra burdens

Practical and efficient, conserves energy

Calm, cool, collected

Brings peace to the workplace

Makes a very good parent

Takes quality time with their children

Family comes first

Strong spiritual leaders

Peaceful and agreeable

Good administrative skills

Good leaders

Good mediators

Tough projects do not worry him

Very good under pressure

Self-sufficient

Has gift of temperance

Gets involved when he feels needed

Has gift of longsuffering

Easy to get along with

Do not offend others

Walks away from arguments

Good listeners

Predictable

Hides real feelings, emotions

Can be selfish, want their way

Can be too compromising

Self-righteous, everyone else is "wrong"

May think they don't need God

Not tidy in their home

Do not discipline well

Not goal oriented

Discourages others

Stay un-involved

Must be nudged to participate

Last one to get involved

Hard to get excited

Tendency to judge others

Teases extroverts - they annoy him

Resists change

Can be sarcastic

Procrastinates

Critical of people who expend energy

Holds grudges

Complacent

Possessive

Miriam

Melancholic

(The Good List and the Bad List)

Strengths of a Melancholic	Weaknesses of a Melancholic
Deep and thoughtful	Moody and depressed
Reserved	Candidate for manic depression
Analytical	Does not forgive easily
Talented, creative	Enjoys being hurt
Artistic, musical	Low self-image
Communes easily with God	Has a false humility
Prayer warriors	Off in another world
Perfectionist	Critical of self and others
Faithful, devoted friend	Self-centered, self examining
Appreciates beauty	Very suspicious
Sensitive	Demands privacy
Self-sacrificing	Too introspective
Conscientious	Feelings of persecution
Idealist	Hypochondriac

Logical	Lingers on past hurts, seems to enjoy it
Peaceful	Broods over things
Agreeable	Absorbed by his thoughts
Good problem solver	Hard to get along with, turns people off
Organized	Pessimistic, remembers negatives
Neat, tidy	Very proud
Great teacher	Can be impractical
Encourages others	Slow to make a decision
Controlled self-discipline	Does not live in the present
Empathetic to others	Selective hearing
Good listeners and counselors	Resentful when not appreciated
Inventive	Too meticulous for children
Have discernment of Spirit	Loses confidence in others
Happy to be in the background	Exasperated by disorder
Longsuffering	Dwells on guilt
Does not get upset easily	Deep need for approval
Avoids conflicts	Sets very high, hard standards
Makes lifelong friends	Hard to please
Open to receiving wisdom	Hard to meet up to his standards
Believes in "letter of the law"	Disapproving
Has controlled self-discipline	Has no tolerance for the undisciplined

The Sanguine

(The Good List and the Bad List)

Strengths of a Sanguine	Weaknesses of a Sanguine
Appealing personality	Compulsive talker
Life of the party	Has loud voice and laugh
Talkative, storyteller	Too happy for some
Good sense of humor	Exaggerates, elaborates
Holds on to listeners	Dwells on trivia
Emotional and demonstrative	Can't remember names
Enthusiastic and expressive	Egotistical
Cheerful and bubbling over	Has restless energy
Loves people	Naïve, gets taken in
Good on stage	Gets angry easily
Sincere heart, wants to give	Controlled by circumstances
Lives in the present	Seems phony to some
Motivates others	Very loud, boisterous
Makes friends easily	Disorganized

Realist

Great salespeople

Entertaining

Optimistic

Tender and compassionate

Energetic

Likes spontaneous activities

Envied by others

Apologizes quickly

Doesn't hold grudges

Creative and colorful

Makes home fun

Trusting

Likes to play

Charms others to work

Thrives on compliments

Inspires others to join

Changeable disposition

Turns disaster into humor

Volunteers for jobs

Looks great on the surface

Sloppy housekeepers

Has trouble listening

Can't relax, always on go

Doesn't follow through

Impulsive

Must be with people

Hates to be alone

Needs to be center stage

Gets angry easily

Makes excuses

Fickle and forgetful

Undisciplined

Cannot say no

Weak willed

Insecure, lack of self- esteem

Interrupts and doesn't listen

Wants to be popular

Dominates conversations

Repeats stories

Forgets obligations

Answers for others

Chapter 14

THE COMPASSIONATE WOMAN—GIVING FROM THE HEART

"And so, as those who have been chosen of God, holy and beloved, put on a heart of compassion" (Colossians 3:12 NASB)

One of the traits of my minister husband is his great heart of compassion and generosity. I'm not sure why, but that was a new concept for me, and at first I didn't understand it. Maybe my lack of empathy for others outside of my own little home came from my poor beginnings. My dad was a tough businessman who had scrambled from his dirt-poor farm beginnings, climbing out of scratching a living on the rocky hillsides of Pennsylvania to being a home builder and fairly wealthy landowner. He wasn't ruthless, but he certainly looked out for himself and his family to survive and get ahead. Tight budgets, hand-me-down clothing, and hard work on the farm influenced my childhood years. It was only after I was an adult that he finally achieved success and lived in a beautiful home on his own lake. I never experienced any of his affluence, so my heritage was: hold on tightly to anything you can—you might need it.

One day early in our marriage, Thomas was counseling a young couple having trouble dealing with a rough situation: the husband was dying of cancer, and the wife was trying to make ends meet as well as deal with it all emotionally. Thomas's response was that in addition to giving them spiritual help, he gave them $100. That is about all we had tucked away. *My* response would have been: "How sad. I feel so bad for them," never thinking of touching our precious nest egg. In fact, when he told me what he had done, I was a little shocked, and thought— and said—"but we might need that money." I'll never forget what he said: "You can never out-give God. He will supply what we need when we need it." And in our 40-some years together since, I have to admit, God has always supplied our needs. I have slowly learned, as I watched God supply every need, but I have never grown a heart as big as my husband's when it comes to giving.

> Blessed is he that considereth the poor: the LORD will deliver him in time of trouble. The LORD will preserve him, and keep him alive; and he shall be blessed upon the earth. (Psalm 41:1,2 KJV)

One such demonstration of God's amazing supply was during Thomas's seminary days. He needed $500 for tuition one semester, and we didn't have it. We knelt together by the couch one Sunday afternoon, and he told God, "Lord, if You want me to go to seminary this semester, we need $500. If you don't want me to, that's fine." Almost as soon as we had finished the prayer, there was a knock on the parsonage door. We opened it to find an older couple on our porch. They gave us an envelope and said, "God told us to give this to you." That's all. They didn't come in to visit or anything. In the envelope was $500 cash.

Another time, later on, Thomas brought home a book for me that he thought I would enjoy. It was all about how to buy real estate when you don't have any money, and since my dad had bought and sold houses and land, he thought I would be interested in it. After reading it, I thought it might be a way to supplement our ministry income and help pay for tuition. I was timid about actually putting the concepts in the book into practice, but Thomas said, "I don't know anything about real estate, but I know how to pray. I'll pray for you, while you go look for a property." So, he prayed, and I drove into the nearby town. I thought I would hunt "for sale" signs and start getting an idea about what was for sale. One of the first streets I went to was in a pretty residential neighborhood, not fancy or expensive, but nice. A white brick house looked like it was just what I would like to buy; it looked solid, not too big, but needed a little TLC—but no for sale sign. I was going to continue driving by it when I felt the nudge to stop. I sat in the car looking at it, and felt again a nudge. "Ask if it is for sale." Where did that thought come from? God? Rather sheepishly, I rang the doorbell and asked the woman if the house was for sale. Well, you guessed it; she had just been thinking of selling it but hadn't done anything about it yet. She was willing to work with me about very little down payment, and we bought our first investment property!

I could go on and on about the ways God supplied our needs, but the important thing is that He did, always. And Thomas was right; it is ok to give all we have if He prompts us to, because He has lots more to give whenever we need it. That frees us up to be a channel of blessing to others in need. It also encourages us to be in touch with Him regularly, because only He knows when and where to give. We don't live under condemnation that we should "give more," or "give it all away." We just try to hear Him as He brings the right situation to us and lets us know what He wants us to do. In the meantime, He lets us also enjoy His bounty.

Compassion is, according to Merriam Webster: "sympathetic consciousness of others' distress together with a desire to alleviate it." It goes beyond what I knew growing up—feeling sorry for them—to where we look for ways to actually help.

Author Helen Andelin says, in *Fascinating Womanhood*,

> Although becoming the Domestic Goddess is our
> prime responsibility [as wives and mothers], it can
> become a narrow existence if continued indefinitely
> with no thought for others. We do owe a certain
> public good to the world, and it is such benevolence
> that enriches a woman's life.

As I read that, I thought of my mother. She spent all her days and nights lovingly providing a great home atmosphere for us nine children. In addition to the normal home chores, she even canned hundreds of jars of food from her huge gardens and orchard, pasteurized milk from her own milk cow, sewed our clothing, and won blue ribbons at the state fair for her incomparable bread and fudge. Yet one memory stands out as amazing: when she made bread for her big hungry brood, she would take one loaf to a widower up the road. As busy as she was, she took time to show compassion for the lonely old man.

Compassion is an important part of our beauty makeover. When we intentionally add compassion to our beauty kit, we will find that it really makes a difference in how beautiful others perceive us. Compassion is better for our beauty than Retinal-A or Botox.

There are many ministries that help the poor and hungry of the world. Sometimes the Lord directs us to give to them, sometimes not. It is really a matter of following the prompting of the Holy Spirit. There are always poor people, and if you just give because they need what you have, your resources are not directed in the best way. Let God be the guide; just be open to His leading, and trust that He will supply what you need.

There is another dimension of compassion that we should consider. Compassion is going beyond just being sorry for someone and then giving money or goods. There is often something even more needed: forgiveness, tenderness, clemency, commiseration, mercy, time. Look at what many valuable things that we have to give!

For instance, a way to give the gift of tender forgiveness might be to overlook man's thoughtless mistakes. Women tend to keep track of events and details, but men are more often late for meals and forget to call. They spend a lot of time or money on their hobbies; they forget important dates and anniversaries; they forget an errand that was important to you. Helen Andelin says, "Your sympathy will make forgiveness easy and will remove a millstone from his neck." Men should not fear to come home and "face the music" of their blunders. They should know you are sweet and forgiving, and they will try even harder to please you! You might think that they will try hard to please you if you are a force to be reckoned with, but the opposite is true. They will eventually give up trying to please someone who is a hard taskmaster, but they will do all they can to try to improve so they can please the sweet one they adore.

Psychologists generally define forgiveness as a conscious, deliberate decision to release feelings of resentment or vengeance toward a person or group who has harmed you, *regardless of whether they actually deserve your forgiveness.* God is good and big-hearted, forgiving us as a free gift. Forgiving others is our free gift to them, as we imitate God and move toward becoming a heavenly woman.

> You're well-known as good and forgiving, bighearted to all who ask for help. Pay attention, GOD, to my prayer; bend down and listen to my cry for help. Every time I'm in trouble I call on you, confident that you'll answer. (Psalm 86:5 MSG)

> Beloved, do not imitate what is evil, but what is good. The one who does good is of God; the one who does evil has not seen God. (3 John 1:11 NASB)

Another gift we can give, as a heavenly woman, is tenderness:

> Be kind to one another, tender-hearted, forgiving
> each other, just as God in Christ also has forgiven
> you. (Ephesians 4:32 NASB)

> Be gentle with one another, sensitive. Forgive one
> another as quickly and thoroughly as God in Christ
> forgave you. (Ephesians 4:32 MSG)

An amazing but often overlooked thing we can give is *clemency*. Wikipedia says clemency is a pardon: "A clemency, a pardon, is a government decision to allow a person to be *absolved of guilt* for an alleged crime or other legal offense, *as if the act never occurred.*" What a gift it is to lift the load of guilt from someone. There are times in a relationship that the offending one is "sorry," and the offended says "that's ok," but still holds the offender as guilty. I have even heard an offended wife remind her spouse of past guilts to "keep him in line." It is so much better to give complete pardon, "as if the act never occurred." We should pair forgiveness with clemency so you can start afresh and go onward in the relationship. Without clemency and forgiveness, you will be stuck in the past. It is God's job to deal with the offending person to help them see their errors, and it is also up to God to deal with them as they grow stronger or even if they might fall into offending again. It is up to us to *trust God* in the situation, and accept their "sorry." Heavenly women, who have a Heavenly Father looking out for them, can afford to give clemency, bringing hope of real change and happiness to all. It might be just the very thing that will motivate the offending person to behold their offense in the blinding light of God's grace, shown through the forgiveness and clemency of their heavenly woman.

Another gift—a blessing—we can give is to just *listen*. Sometimes a sick or sad or poor person just needs to feel that someone will take time to listen to them and "feel their pain." When we take time to listen to someone, they feel *validated*, they feel that they matter. Remember that everyone who crosses your path in life is one Jesus died for. He died for "the just and the unjust." *They may not know it yet,* but *we* know it, and we can learn to treat them as someone Jesus loves. We may be the first step in their feeling that they are worth something—to you, because of what God has done in your life, and to God because of what He has done for them.

> To sum up, all of you be harmonious, sympathetic, brotherly, kindhearted, and humble in spirit; not returning evil for evil or insult for insult, but giving a blessing instead; for you were called for the very purpose that you might inherit a blessing. (I Peter 3:8,9 NASB)

So, compassion, as evidenced by so many diverse gifts, is something for us heavenly women to ponder and endeavor to include in our lives. It is a wonderful thing to show compassion, first to those God has given us in our own family, and then to the world outside our own little family spheres, as an essential part of spreading the Gospel. This is the Good News of Jesus. As we have received compassion from the Lord, so we can pass it on.

A couple of years back, I was in the hospital, and felt like an insignificant number on the list of patients waiting on procedures. Stripped of my own clothes and my dignity, dressed in the thin cold uniform of the hospitalized, I lay with needle in my arm and tubes and wires tangled around me. Among the many efficient and kind professionals who came in and out of my cubicle, one stood out. Her warm smile and sympathetic eyes seemed different. She noticed how cold I was and produced a heated blanket. She asked if anyone had explained all about what would happen before, during, and after the procedure I was awaiting, and I said no. She explained it and asked if I had any concerns she could address. Just the fact that she slowed down and took time to really look at me and listen to me validated me as a human being again, not just a number on the list. She cared. I said to her, "You are so tender—why are you so different from the others?" She smiled an April smile. Her answer was so simple, so sweet: "Jesus loves me." How pure her witness was, because she had shown compassion. Had I not already met Jesus and knew He loved me too, I would have been ready to find out all about this Jesus. She was ready to give an account for the hope in her heart, just as Peter instructs us all:

> But sanctify Christ as Lord in your hearts, always being ready to make a defense to everyone who asks you to give an account for the hope that is in you, yet with gentleness and reverence; (1 Peter 3:8,9 NASB)

LIVING IT:

Listen to God for guidance as to how to show compassion in its different forms. Give forgiveness to your mate, your family, your associates if they offend you. Look for ways to be kind, to pray for people, to have a heart to help others, to be tenderhearted. Open your eyes and your heart. Maybe your purse.

Here is the power part: especially give out compassion and forgiveness and tenderness when others don't deserve it. Then your goodness will show up even more against their ungodliness and you will be letting your light shine. Just be careful that you don't show mercy in a way that is just a show-off, puffed up thing. Don't wear your kindness and mercy like a priestly robe, proud of yourself, but as a humble sackcloth garment, proud that God had mercy on you, and that you can pass it on.

Find a ministry such as COMPASSION INTERNATIONAL, or a local food bank or pregnancy center or whatever godly ministry you are interested in and look up what they do. Ask the Lord if there is a ministry that He knows is something you will get joy from working with, either giving money or time or blankets or whatever. The women of times past "rolled bandages" during wars, or took hot soup to sick poor people. Just remember the old adage that charity begins at home, so don't neglect your husband or family to "minister" to the world. Mark 7:11 similarly says that we shouldn't neglect our own family to do religious ministry. Because of their sympathetic feminine nature, women have to watch out for that!

FOR FUN:

Watch the Liam Neeson version of the movie "Les Miserables." Notice how the old bishop's forgiveness of the convict changes the convict's life. (Les Misérables is a 1998 film adaptation of Victor Hugo's 1862 novel of the same name, directed by Bille August. It stars Liam Neeson, Geoffrey Rush, Uma Thurman, and Claire Danes.)

Chapter 15

THE SPEAKING WOMAN:
FLUENT IN LANGUAGES OF LOVE

Je t'aime, mon amour (I love you, my dear)

One of the first things that attracted me to my husband Thomas was his charming English accent, back before I had actually met him. He had preached a sermon as a guest preacher in a church nearby, and it was so memorable that I can still remember his interesting voice and the subject more than forty years later.

When I met and fell in love with him, I was still charmed by his speaking, whether he was preaching to a crowd or just talking to me. He sang too, but interestingly he had no English accent when he sang: he was Jim Reeves, Bill Gaither, and himself, all rolled into a smooth, soothing sound. (He actually did a beautiful recording in Nashville, many years ago! The album was entitled "Moments.")

In fact, Thomas was one of the backup singers on stage with Bill Gaither once. I will never forget it, for more reasons than the honor it was for Thomas to be there with Bill himself. As they were practicing before the concert, I was sitting in the front row of the empty auditorium, with my 35 millimeter camera, back when we used actual rolls of film. I wanted to have picture proof that Thomas sang with the one and only Bill Gaither! Bill came over to me and said, "My photographer doesn't seem to have shown up—would you take photos for me, and send them later?" SURE, forever! I was so proud to be asked. After the concert started, I shot 36 photos, since my rolls of film were 36 exposures. When the concert was nearly over, and I was going to put a new roll of film in the camera, something weird happened—it advanced again. How could that be? I tried another shot, and it advanced again. And again. My heart felt that sinking feeling when you realize you've made a great blunder. *I had forgotten to put film in the camera at all*, so the advance dial was just turning, not winding film. I had also brought my old mini-quick-shoot type of camera, and took pictures, but I knew that with the stage lighting and distance, they would be poor. (They were awful, but I did get proof of the concert with a blurry and shaded photo of Bill with his arm around Thomas!) I was so embarrassed, I couldn't face Bill Gaither to tell him what I had done, and never even wrote to him. I am still ashamed that I didn't at least tell him. If I had communicated, he might have even laughed. I'm so sorry, Bill!

Since we Americans say we "speak English," I assumed Thomas and I spoke the same language. I was in for a real shock the first time I met his English family, when shortly after our wedding we traveled to his hometown in Halesowen, England. His sisters all came to meet me at his parents' home, and as we sat around the "lounge" (living room), I couldn't understand one word they said. It was the real deal English, with a "Black Country" twist. I was at a complete loss, and had to keep turning to Thomas and whisper, "What did they say?" After many visits and years, my ear is tuned to their speech, and I don't even hear the difference anymore, and I have learned that a cookie is a "biscuit," a car hood is "bonnet," the restroom is a "loo," a raincoat is a "mac," and if the English say they are thirsty, don't offer them a glass of water; they mean they want a cup of tea.

Thomas and I communicated pretty well, but it took some time to decipher what each other was really meaning. Words are not all that are involved; there is so much in each language that is culturally understood. For instance, in England, one speaks what one means and just says it. In America, we sometimes are shocked at such forthrightness, and we sugarcoat things. The English can seem rude at times to Americans, and Americans can seem vague. If you ask an Englishman if he wants to do a certain thing and he does not, he assumes you really want to know, and he just says, "No." If you ask an American if they want to do something, and they don't, they tend to try to find an excuse that avoids saying no, because "no" seems rude. Even in marriages between people of the same culture and language, poor communication is one of the main issues that bring people to a marriage counselor.

I hear that in some Oriental cultures, it is considered rude to even speak directly to a business associate about a project; it is expected that you will speak to another peripheral person and who will in turn convey your message. I haven't been to the Orient, so I can't say for sure. In the movie ANNA AND THE KING, the famous British school teacher Anna Leonowens was offended when the Siamese court asked her personal questions when she wanted to conduct official business. They explained that in Siam it was rude to skip the personal step, yet in American culture, it seems rude to ask personal questions in a business situation.

And so we realize that communication and language is complicated. We can say what we mean, but if we say it in a language that others don't understand, they will not get the message.

There are, perhaps, a great many kinds of languages in the world, and no kind is without meaning. If then I do not know the meaning of the language, I will be to the one who speaks a barbarian, and the one who speaks will be a barbarian to me. (1 Corinthians 14:10 NASB)

Dr. Gary Chapman's famous book, *The Five Love Languages*, was a No.1 New York Times Best Seller. With over 12 million copies sold, it has transformed countless relationships. Aspiring to be heavenly women, we need to learn these five languages if we want to show love to those in our families and those in our world. Don't panic—these languages are really easy to learn. And fun! We will learn them together this week. But first, let me illustrate what Dr. Chapman's love languages can mean for a couple.

A young woman came to Thomas for marriage counseling several years ago. She loved her husband, but they had drifted apart and he had moved out. She was a smart, pretty, vivacious (and choleric temperament) gal who was determined to save her marriage and was ready to do something about it (again a choleric action). She came for counseling for nearly a year before she could convince her husband to come; he wasn't one to rush into things (he was phlegmatic/sanguine temperament). It turned out that even though they loved each other, each felt unloved. Here's the good part: they were speaking two different love languages, but once they learned each other's language, they made great progress. Her love language was not French (je t'aime, mon amour), Chinese (我爱你), not Spanish (Te quiero), but it was *"acts of service."* His love language was *"physical touch."* So the 12 years they were married, when he wanted to just cuddle on the sofa and watch a movie together to show her how much he loved her, it was like he was saying *je t'aime*. She didn't receive the message, "I love you." In fact, she thought he was saying, "I'm lazy. I don't care about you." In counseling, when they learned to speak the language of love that each could correctly understand, the "light went on," and they "got it"! She said, "If he wants me to feel loved, he should vacuum the house for me when I'm busy." *That kind of love, "acts of service," she understood.* And he said if she would just sit down with him in a relaxed and cozy way, he would feel loved, in his "physical touch" language. They learned to speak the language of love that the other understood, and their marriage was reborn.

What are these 5 Love Languages, you ask? Very simply, they are:

- receiving gifts
- quality time
- words of affirmation
- acts of service (devotion)
- physical touch

RECEIVING GIFTS:

Just about everybody perceives gift giving as an expression of love. There is something inside the human mind that says if you love someone, you will give things to them.

However, for those whose love language is "receiving gifts," it is *the* thing that makes them feel most loved. They don't look for thanks, they don't look for you to vacuum for them, and they don't look for cuddling to feel loved. It doesn't have to be expensive or elaborate; it is literally the thought that counts. Even flowers from a field mean a lot to a person whose primary love language is "receiving gifts." Birthdays and anniversaries are really important to those who speak this language, and "no occasion" gifts make them feel incredibly treasured.

If you are on a business trip, or even a shopping trip, and your spouse speaks the "receiving gifts" language, make it a point to bring them something, even if it is just their favorite candy bar.

It wouldn't do to skip the gift and hurry home to mow the grass or take the garbage out, because even though those acts of service would be appreciated, they wouldn't be translated as "I love you."

QUALITY TIME:

If your spouse's love language is "quality time," you need to do just that: make quality time for them. If you put your book or magazine down and look into their eyes as they talk to you, they interpret that little action as saying, "I love you."

Quality time is not the same thing as quantity of time. We all have many responsibilities, and if the family is hungry and we are cooking supper, we may not be able to drop everything and gaze into the spouse's eyes at that moment. But do try to find 20 minutes to give a "quality time" spouse undivided attention, where you look at them and listen, and converse. That 20 minutes will be like putting money in their bank of love, and they will feel loved. You will reap rewards too, because when a spouse feels loved, they also start feeling more loving towards you.

That goes for any of your children who speak "quality time" love language. They thrive on "quality time" when you get on their level and really look and listen. Some kids don't need or want that as much as they want solitude and quiet, or maybe they would rather discover that you bought their favorite treat when you were at the store. A heavenly woman makes it her business to learn to speak the correct language for each member of her family.

WORDS OF AFFIRMATION:

Simply saying, "Thank you for taking the garbage out, Honey," or "I'm so glad you mowed the lawn—it looks so nice," is interpreted as "I love you," to a spouse whose love language is "words of affirmation." It is a very easy language to learn.

If your spouse's primary love language is "words of affirmation," your spoken praise and appreciation will be like warm spring showers on cold, dry soil. Before long, you will see new life sprouting in your marriage as your spouse responds to your words of love. The same thing works for children and relatives (and neighbors and co-workers, if you can determine their love language, which is a bit harder if they aren't working on it with you).

My secondary love language is "words of affirmation." Words in general are part of that language: I have loved it that Thomas would write love verses to me. Sometimes he would bring his guitar into the kitchen while I was cooking and sing love songs to me. To me, that was wonderful. However, to a person who spoke "acts of service," that might be annoying to hear love songs when what they really wanted was help in the kitchen!

A woman I know found out too late that her husband's love language was "words of affirmation." For years, she had used words to tear him down. She often said he didn't know how to run his business. She said he didn't do the lawns like her dad did. She said he didn't spend enough time with her. She said he was lazy and didn't do enough around the house. Words, words, words, not of affirmation, but of destruction. His secondary language was "receiving gifts," so he assumed that she would understand that his generous provision of best furniture, clothes, houses, etc. while he used words to praise her beauty would say "I love you." Not so. Her primary language was "quality time," and her secondary language was "acts of service," so all his financial provision and gifts and words meant little to her, and she felt unloved. Unfortunately, they are divorced. I think if they could have learned to speak each other's languages, they would still be married today.

If you find out that the reason you and your mate are not

getting along is that your love languages have been damaged in some way, that can be a serious problem. Not too serious for God to fix, but you will need to make a serious project of praying about it and doing all you can to remedy the situation. For instance, if a husband's primary love language is "quality time," and the wife has for years left him too much time on his own without her presence while she pursued her own goals, career, hobbies, horses, or whatever, he may have his need-bank of quality time so depleted that he shuts down his feelings for her. Somewhere he hardens himself to cover the pain and finds things to do or people to be with so that eventually he doesn't even want her around. Then she discovers the love languages and realizes that she has damaged him by not giving him quality time, so she tries to suddenly be in his presence, wants to go to his hobbies with him, or plans events with him. If the damage has been done too long, he may not want to be with her at all, so no amount of her trying to fill his need for quality time works. Without the intervention of prayer and God's healing, that couple either lives a lifetime of miserable marriage, or they divorce. It could be the other way around, where the husband does too many things with his sports or hunting or car buddies, and the wife feels left out. At first she may pine for his attention and complain that he is never home or that they don't do things together. If it goes on too many years, she may build an emotional wall to cover her hurt, and go the other extreme of being glad he is gone so she can do what she wants. If he sees that he has damaged her need for quality time, he will try to do things with her and stay home more, but she is annoyed at his presence. That takes a lot of prayer; but we have heard of couples that have come back from the brink of splitting up and now have united and fulfilling marriages.

ACTS OF SERVICE:

If "acts of service" is your spouse's primary love language, about the only way they will really hear "I love you" is when you do something to help them. If a husband tells his wife "I love you," while sitting on the sofa as she washes dishes, she will not hear it at all. Inside, she would be thinking, "If he really loved me, he would be here helping me do the dishes." Often the wife will think, "He is just lazy and thoughtless." Really, if his love language is not acts of service, it might not really occur to him to help.

You do hear of husbands who bring expensive gifts to their wives, thinking that will convince her that he loves her; but if she speaks "acts of service," she will probably think he is just wasting money or trying to get on her good side. It doesn't translate into "I love you." The husband may finally be confused and say she is hard to please. She is probably thinking that his words and gifts don't mean anything.

For the spouse or children who speak "acts of service," keep in mind the old phrase, "actions speak louder than words." Simple acts of service will fill up their love tank and it will pay off in their happiness and in how they feel towards you.

PHYSICAL TOUCH:

Research has shown how important it is for babies to be touched. Long before babies learn the words of love, they feel loved by being cuddled and rocked. Well-adjusted children are shown physical love as they are nurtured in the home, and it is natural for them as adults to reach out to a mate for physical touch.

In marriage, there is naturally physical attraction and intimacy, no matter what love languages are spoken by each mate. However, for the spouse who speaks the language of "physical touch," no amount of gifts or acts of service or great flowery words say "I love you" like simple touching. In fact, simple touch speaks louder to the person whose love language is physical touch than sexual touch, because in marriage, sex is a given. A brief touch on the shoulder as the mate passes by, or holding hands as you walk together, or an arm around you as you sit together—all these are like gold to the one whose language is physical touch, and are translated "I love you."

My own primary language of love is "physical touch," with my secondary language of love being "words of affirmation." So heaven for me is if hubby gives me a back rub and says some words like "I love how soft your hair is." Touch and words. That does it for me. I don't need diamonds, I don't need flowers, I don't need a new car or grand furniture. I found that I don't even really need quality time. When Thomas was in seminary and had to be gone all week every week, I was ok with that. I had lots to do with the children, my garden, my art, whatever. I was just glad to see him on Friday. Some wives complain if the husband works too much or is gone a lot, but they probably are speaking "quality time" language. It all works once you learn the right language.

When my husband took the 5 Languages test again recently, I was surprised and pleased. I already knew that "quality time" was important to him, but I didn't know that "physical touch" was his secondary language, tied with "words of affirmation." Early on in our marriage, I realized that even though "quality time" wasn't near the top of my list and I could go days without feeling left out or lonely, I found that he needed time with me, time where I wasn't looking down at crafts or books or anything—just looking at him and conversing. As I learned about the language of "quality time," we bonded in a great way. But the surprise and delight about the test results now was that all the years of his holding my hand and touching in the kitchen, writing verses of poetry to me, saying nice compliments to me, were not just him learning to speak my "physical touch" and "words of affirmation" languages, but were straight out of his own natural languages too. That is even nicer. However, even if we aren't natural-born speakers of a language, learning it for the sake of the other is a great work. Speaking languages of our mate and family members so that they translate it as "I love you" is powerful and wonder-working.

Love is so important. It is the desire of our hearts to be loved, and that is why it is so wonderful when we find that God loves us unconditionally with complete commitment. That is also why we seek a mate who will love us, also unconditionally with complete commitment. When we don't feel loved, our hopes and dreams are dashed. I might say that even though we *are* loved, if we don't *perceive it as love*, it is death to us. Look at what the Apostle Paul writes to the Corinthian church:

> If I speak with the tongues of men and of angels, but do not have love, I have become a noisy gong or a clanging cymbal. If I have the gift of prophecy, and know all mysteries and all knowledge; and if I have all faith, so as to remove mountains, but do not have love, I am nothing. And if I give all my possessions to feed the poor, and if I surrender my body to be burned, but do not have love, it profits me nothing.

> Love is patient, love is kind and is not jealous; love does not brag and is not arrogant, does not act unbecomingly; it does not seek its own, is not provoked, does not take into account a wrong suffered, does not rejoice in unrighteousness, but rejoices with the truth; bears all things, believes all things, hopes all things, endures all things.

> Love never fails. (I Corinthians 14:1—8 NASB)

Heavenly women make love their aim, and one of the things they must learn is to speak the language of love that will actually be *received as love*. You might say, "Why do *I* have to be the one to learn these languages? Why not my mate, or my kids? Who will fill *my* needs?" Good questions. But you know the answer. *You* are the one who is aspiring to heavenly ways. If you are clever enough to teach your mate and your kids what their languages are *and* what your languages are, it will be the best of all. But even if they do not cooperate, you are the one who understands, and the one who will be able to make a real difference. And think of it this way: even if your love language is, say, "physical touch," but your mate's is "acts of service," you can be smart enough to translate what acts of service he does for you into the words "I love you." After all, that is the desire of our hearts: to be loved.

LIVING IT:

Take the Love Languages Personal Profile test which you can find free at the 5 Love Languages website, https://5lovelanguages.com, or in Dr. Chapman's book, THE FIVE LOVE LANGUAGES, and see what your love languages are, primary and secondary. If you tell your spouse you are hoping to understand him better so you can meet his needs, he will probably take the test too. If he doesn't, you can "take it for him," surmising what his answers might be. Then try to get fluent in his languages! Try to make a difference by your understanding of his languages and translating his acts into "I love you." If you are single, think of your family and co-workers, and see if you can understand their languages better.

FOR FUN:

Write in your notebook what *your* primary and secondary languages are, so you can know yourself better. It is part of the new heavenly you. Even if you are alone in life at this period of time, rejoicing in the wonders of how God designed YOU is a comforting and calming thing, giving the feeling you might have felt as a small child when your mother brushed your hair and lovingly told you how pretty you were. (At least that's what I like to *imagine!* My mother had 9 children, and I was a middle child with hardly any hair to brush.)

Chapter 16

THE CHARMING WOMAN—
PLEASANT AND LIKABLE

When I was only 17, my dream was to be an airline hostess, so I enrolled in an airline hostess course and went off to Kansas City, which was the hub of the airline industry at that time. One of the fascinating parts of it was the charm course. In those days, it was still OK for women to want to be pretty and charming. The Airline hostesses were trained to be pleasant in actions and in appearance, as ambassadors for the airline, whose goal was to make the passengers feel welcome and cared for and to have a positive travel experience. We were taught how to be ladylike and pleasant; in a word, "charming."

Jump ahead to the current time. I had some of my grandchildren over and they were telling me about a new Star Wars movie. They wanted me to look it up on my smart TV to see the trailer for it. I was not surprised by what I saw, but I was still very saddened to see that the main figure of this movie was a powerful woman. And I don't mean powerful because she understood and used the powerful feminine gifts God gave to only women—no, she excelled in everything masculine. Her clothes were men's military uniforms and her hair was a mess. If looks could kill, she wouldn't have needed the light saber. How I mourned for

Princess Leia who back in the 70s wore her beautiful white gown and had her hair all coiffed prettily, and needed rescued, like the damsels in distress of old who waited for their knights in shining armor. OK, she *was* a smart, active member of her senate as well as princess of her planet in the original Star Wars movie, but very feminine. As the later Star Wars movies came out, she was changed into more of a masculine fighter. That's part of our current culture, that women can do anything a man can do, and probably better. (Recently I broke my knee in an accident, and when researching about it, I thought it was interesting to learn that broken knees and torn knee ligaments happen more in sports to females than males, "because their structure is more delicate and their muscles have a different makeup which makes them prone to injury.")

I guess you know by now having been in the study with me so long that I think in our heart of hearts, most of us women still want to be rescued by that handsome knight in shining armor. I also think that in men's heart of hearts, *no men* want to be rescued by a fiercely strong, combative woman. Our current culture has things really twisted around and mixed up, and then people wonder why there is so much dissatisfaction in relationships. I say that any woman has a right to be as masculine and independent as she wants; she should just realize that it is incompatible with finding a sweet, protected place in a man's heart.

I'll let you in on a little secret: the gals who are charming would be more of what a man would, in his heart of hearts, wish to marry. He may enjoy playing around with a feisty and dangerous woman, but that's not who he would like to have as his life companion and mother to his children. We don't have to go to charm school, but if we want to be heavenly women, it would make sense that we would look at things that help us be more charming women. We can learn how to adapt what might be naturally unpleasant ways to pleasant ways. Webster says "charming" is "pleasant, likeable." Even if you feel that marriage is not for you at this time in your life, think of all those around you in your life who would enjoy your company if you are charming. Who doesn't prefer to be around pleasant, likable people?

> You are altogether beautiful, my darling; there is no flaw in you. (Song of Songs 4:7 EHV)

And, lest we forget, we are not just "people." We are women! And women have their own kind of charm. While it is true that you can say that a certain man is a "charming young man," whatever makes him charming will be quite different from the way a woman could be charming.

> Her ways are pleasant ways, and all her paths are peace. (Proverbs 3:17 NASB)
>
> And sweetness of speech increases persuasiveness. (Proverbs 16:21, NASB)
>
> The heart of the wise teaches his mouth, and adds persuasiveness to his lips. Pleasant words are a honeycomb, sweet to the soul and healing to the bones. (Proverbs 16:23,24 NASB)

If we were to go to what used to be called "charm school," or in more elite circles, "finishing school," there are a variety of subjects. The goal is to learn to live in a beautiful way, a charming, pleasant and feminine way. Let's look at some of them.

Looks:

Although a woman doesn't have to be pretty to be charming, it is generally considered part of it. A charming woman is feminine.

Think of the original Princess Leia. She was pretty, and there was no mistaking her for one of the guys.

Today women wear pants almost exclusively, but there is a lot to be said about dresses or skirts. Try wearing a dress to the grocery store next time. It makes a difference in how men treat you. Last week I went to the grocery store in a dress and I was buying a big heavy turkey as well as quite a few other items to get ready for a holiday meal. Since some back surgery, I have not been able to lift very much, and as I stood with the loaded cart at the back of my van with the hatch open, I was in a bit of a quandary. I should've planned better and taken Thomas along with me—but there I was, tugging at the turkey and trying to figure a way to coax him to the top of the cart and tip into my van. A man (with his wife, just so you don't get the wrong idea) stepped up and asked if I could use a hand. It was just what I needed. I think a dress gets the attention of men in a protective way, seeing if we need help. (Let's assume the dress is modest, not something to attract a man in the wrong way.)

If you are married, you probably already know the difference in the way your husband treats you when you're wearing a dress. There's just something about the dress that accentuates the difference between masculinity and femininity, calling forth the innate protective, strong side of man. Don't we want to be treated gently and kindly, and don't we like it when the husband offers to open doors for us or do yucky jobs for us? Then we should look to our part of helping him feel protective towards us.

When my boys were little, I noticed that even they treated me differently around the house if I wore a dress. They seemed to offer to help me more and show respect.

I am not saying that we gals can't wear trousers, because it is so practical. I think that feminine pants can actually be very attractive. Sometimes they can be cute, sometimes they can be classy, but they should always say, "this is a girl, not a guy."

Another thing they teach you in charm school is to have

pretty hair. I know that sometimes it is tempting to just have a hairstyle that is easy to take care of even if it is boring or unflattering. However, it is much more pleasant to those around you (and don't forget that charming means *pleasant*) if your hair is feminine, clean, and well taken care of. You will feel better about yourself, too. If you aren't taking about 30 minutes a day on your dressing, hair and makeup, you probably aren't looking as great as you could. If you spend more than 30 minutes, you might be spending more time on your looks than you need to for everyday situations.

I might add that most men prefer long hair. If you have extremely thin fine hair like I do it may be that short hair might actually look more attractive, since it could be stringy and untidy when long. I have worn mine short a lot of my life, but lately I have let it grow out, not to wear straggling around my shoulders, but in some kind of up-do, even at times with a hair extension bun. But whether you can wear your hair short or long, try to find the most attractive style for you, for your face shape, for your personality type, and whatever makes you look your feminine best. If you have very fine hair, you can find lots of ways to not just let it be limp, which is not attractive. There are hair thickener lotions, root pump lotions and more. One of the newer trends is the dry shampoo spray, which is a real time-saver because you can go from having to wash your hair every day or so to sometimes up to a week and still have it look good. It is a great volume builder too. Try different products to see what works best—you are worth it. Be the best woman you can be.

As to looking the best you can be, do conceal problem areas. If we are getting more "mature," consider a turtleneck or scarf or ropes of jewelry to hide a neck that is aging. It was once said of Katherine Hepburn when she was in her 80s that she didn't show skin, but she *looked like* she could if she wanted to. Other ideas: swingy skirts cover too heavy thighs, sleeves cover arms that are scrawny or heavy, tights or leggings cover veined legs. You get the picture.

Of course, there is makeup concealer too—for dark circles or dark pigment around the eyes. I'm not one who advocates much makeup; I think the best makeup for a ladylike appearance just "makes up" for what is deficient. For instance, I have absolutely no cheek color and no lip color, so I look best adding a little to those areas. In fact, if someone sees me without either lip color or cheek color, they usually say, "Are you feeling ok?" No need to worry them about my health, right? I used to have nice heavy eyebrows and didn't wear any brow pencil, but with age they have sort of faded or bailed out, so they need a little help. We do have to be careful, though, because the more mature we get, too much makeup looks like we are trying too hard to be a kid again. Some experts advise us to lighten our shade of lip and cheek color one shade every 10 years. I have found it to be good advice. Remember our chapter on color earlier: wearing your God-ordained colors (Psalm 139) will bring out beauty with very little makeup.

Thinking about color, remember to find your best colors for clothing. Among your best, I encourage you to find your very favorite ones, and build a simple, classic wardrobe around those "signature" colors. They will mix and match and you will need less clothing. Dressing is faster, and everything in your closet will look good on you. Even your "garden clothes" or housework clothes should be in your prettiest colors—why look like a drudge in boring gray or mud colors while working hard, when you can have pink or pale blue or whatever looks feminine and charming.

Even in your own color palette, limit how much bright color and prints you use, and avoid too trendy clothing. It looks expensive and classic to wear neutrals like beige, gray, cream, black, navy, white with just a bit of color, in simple style lines. Your clothing should frame *you*, not detract from you. When you are buying clothing, avoid buying things just because they have amazing prints or details; you don't want your clothes to "arrive" before you do.

Here is an easy trick, and it's like having a personal wardrobe consultant: find attractive pictures of a celebrity with your body shape, to learn what styles and combinations would look good on you. You don't have to agonize over whether you are "pear," "apple," "triangle" or whatever shapes. Very simply, are you curvy or more straight? One thing you can do is an Internet search for the celebrity with a shape like yours and click "images." You can get lots of ideas there of ways to combine your different clothing pieces and shoes for a great look. Try on your own pants, skirts, dresses, vests, jackets, etc., in different combinations and take phone photos of combos that you like. Save them to a new "album" on your phone labeled "clothing outfits," and then you have an instant resource to fall back on when you are stuck about what to put on. Saves time, and you'll look great! (You also might find when you see the picture that some of your favorite outfits don't actually look as good on your frame as you thought, and it might be time to give those things away.)

Elegant ladies wear clothing that is not too tight or revealing. (Remember, we don't want to give men the wrong ideas!) She tries to wear appropriate clothes: appropriate for the event, and appropriate for her age. However, just because we are maturing doesn't mean we can't wear current fashions—just not tasteless or trendy fashions. Do Internet searches for celebrities your own age who look elegant, and see that they are not dowdy and oldish, but also not following the teen trends.

Ladies have pretty hands. Don't ignore your hands. We heavenly women work hard, but use rubber gloves. Use lotions. Stop biting or picking nails. Smooth and shape your nails; a hint is to keep an emery board in the kitchen drawer and by your TV chair as well as in your bathroom. Jojoba oil has very tiny molecules, and if rubbed into your nails and buffed, the nails will start to get pink and shiny and pretty. Once they start to be healthy, you may find that you don't want to interfere with their health with nail polish or artificials. But if you want to wear nail polish, use nude or blush polish if you want look classy. Leave the black and blood red to the teenagers who are trying to get attention.

All your attention to your beauty can be pulled down by some unladylike habits like cracking knuckles, twisting hair or slouching. Elegant ladies learn good posture. The old charm school training we had in airline hostess school was to walk with a book on our heads to learn to keep good posture and balance. It is still a good practice if you tend to slouch. Another way to help with posture is to imagine a helium balloon fastened to your head, just pulling you up. That automatically aligns your neck and back and shoulders.

Finishing schools teach the ladylike way to sit. On a straight chair, sit two thirds of the way on the seat and sit with back straight. Legs should be crossed at ankles, not the knees. Knees should be together. When you get up, have one leg behind the other and push up with the back leg gently and then as you rise, put your weight onto the front leg and it will be very graceful. To sit down, do the reverse: put one foot behind the other and put your weight on the back foot as you sit down. Get in and out of cars by swiveling with both legs together and swing both legs to the ground together.

Heavenly women avoid aggressive gestures. Examples are carelessly slamming doors instead of gently closing them, using a stomping gait, a strong tone of voice, or other masculine gestures. Soften up. Proactively teach yourself to be gentler.

Charming ladies do not bring their drama to someone else's event. If you are having an altercation with your mate or with a friend, don't take it into the public arena. Don't bring your negative emotions or negative speaking into public because it's not appropriate and definitely not like a heavenly woman. It is not attractive to be in a bad mood when in other people's company. I remember one of my relatives, who happened to be a melancholic temperament, many times came to family events acting very quiet and upset. She was usually still mad after having a fight with her husband, and it was embarrassing for the rest of us. My mother, always such a lady, taught us that ladies "don't air their dirty laundry in public."

> Let no corrupting talk come out of your mouths, but only such as is good for building up, as fits the occasion, that it may give grace to those who hear. (Ephesians 4:29 ESV)

Voice:

Speaking of my mother, she used to say that ladies shouldn't yell, or they would sound like a "fishwife," *whatever that is.* It doesn't sound good though, does it? I decided to look it up, and it means "a coarse-mannered woman who is prone to shouting." Not heavenly. I purchased a little hand bell, and taught the family that when I wanted them to come for meals or something, I would ring the little bell. No more opening the door and shouting for all the kids and the neighborhood to hear.

> Gracious words are like a honeycomb, sweetness to the soul and health to the body. (Proverbs 16:24 ESV)

Most of us moms are guilty of yelling at our children from time to time, but if we are looking to become more like a heavenly woman, this is something that we should pay attention to. It's not enough to say, "Well, that's just the way my voice is. I'm loud." Just because something comes naturally to us doesn't mean it is ideal. Just as we learned in the study of personality and temperament types, there is a good list and a bad list. There are things that we should cultivate in our personality type and things that we should avoid. There are things that we should change to rise above what comes naturally.

> A gentle tongue is a tree of life, but perverseness in it breaks the spirit. (Proverbs 15:4 ESV)

> The mind governed by the flesh is death, but the mind governed by the Spirit is life and peace. (Romans 8:6 NIV)

As heavenly women, we are reaching heavenward, trying to be the best version of ourselves. It can be hard work, but we are not alone. Our Lord has promised to send us a helper.

> I will send you the Helper from the Father. The Helper is the Spirit. (John 15:26 ERV)

When we want to do God's work here on earth, we ask the Holy Spirit to help us be what we could not be naturally. We want to live supernaturally!

> But I say, walk by the Spirit, and do not gratify the desires of the flesh. For the desires of the flesh are against the Spirit, and the desires of the Spirit are against the flesh; for these are opposed to each other, to prevent you from doing what you would. But if you are led by the Spirit you are not under the law. (Galatians 5:16—18 NASB)

Look at the last line above in the Galatians passage: "you are *led*," you don't *follow*. Think of being a railroad car (a pretty one) being led by the locomotive engine. It not only leads you, but uses its own strength to get you where you need to go. It is not like the pace car in the Indianapolis 500 race that is just out front showing you the way and seeing who can follow.

Heavenly women avoid slang or vulgar words. For instance, she would not say that she has to go to the bathroom or to the loo when she is at a restaurant with others, She would just say, "Would you please excuse me for a moment?" and slip away to the ladies' room. It only makes sense that a heavenly woman does not swear. She uses correct grammar. Another thing that they teach you in charm school is to be careful that your laugh is sweet and happy and bubbly, not cackling or jarring. It will be different for each heavenly woman, as befits their own personality, but in any event it should not be loud and harsh. Maybe that's how a fishwife laughs, I don't know.

Here is a hidden minefield that we might be unaware of in our own lives: make sure that you are not dominating conversation. The next time you're in a group or at a dinner, pay attention to how much *you* talk compared to the others. You may find that you are more of a talker than you should be, and you need to learn to step back a little and ask questions and let others talk. See if you are thinking of what *you* will jump in and say as soon as there is an opening. You might be surprised. Instead, let the person who is talking shine; give them your attention and ask them about their subject.

Etiquette:

Finishing schools teach table etiquette—it is really easy, and you will enjoy the confidence you will have if you learn it. There are not a lot of rules, and they will help you be up to any occasion. Probably the most important of all, before you even learn a few basic rules of etiquette, is the common sense one of "eating like a lady." A heavenly woman should learn to take small bites and not eat as though she is starving. When you are out eating at a restaurant, try to eat less than you might at home, because it looks unladylike to heap up your plate and eat "like a farmhand."

Remember, we aspire to be heavenly *women*, not *men*. You might want to have a little something to eat before you leave home so you aren't "ravenous."

Here are the simple basic etiquette rules that will see you through most formal dinners:

- If there's a cloth napkin, you pick it up and lay it across your lap. Lift it to dab your mouth gently as needed and return it to your lap.
- If there is an array of silverware, you simply use the outermost piece first and work your way in with different courses. For instance, the salad fork will be the farthest fork to the left, and the salad is served first in America. Then comes the entree and you use the next fork for that. Silverware lying horizontally at the top of the plate is for the dessert course, so you leave them for last.
- Small Plates to the left of your big plate are for bread and butter or sometimes a salad. Drinks are to the upper right of your plate.

That's basically all there is to being comfortable in the most elegant dinner setting. In addition to the simple rules, here are some guidelines to put you over the top in heavenly social behavior. There are some commonsense things to pay attention to, of course, like finish swallowing the bite of food before speaking. That's another good reason to take small bites! Don't wash down bites of food with liquids.

Cell phones should be invisible, and you should never take calls unless urgent. If you are expecting an important call, apologize to those you are with ahead of time. It is rude to talk on the phone when you are in company. You should check your phone only when you go to the restroom. Other than that, don't even lay it on the table. Put it in your bag.

Be respectful by keeping social appointments and be on time.

If you know being late is necessary, let the host know ahead of time and then call or text the same day as the event and remind them that you are looking forward to coming but have to be late. Also, leave on time. Keep goodbyes short.

Miscellaneous tips for heavenly women: slouching is disrespectful; sitting up and looking alertly at the person who is talking to you shows them you are interested in them and what they are saying. It has been said that small people talk about people, average people talk about things, and great people talk about events or ideas. Be cautious. Refrain from getting sucked into talking about others. You can nod slightly—not agreeing but *acknowledging that you are listening*, then steer the conversation in a more positive direction. Don't dominate the conversation. Ask others about their kids, trip, etc. (Later that day use phone notes to remind you to check on them if some event is to happen in their lives so you can text them on that day.)

Don't use slang or profanity if you want to sound like a lady. Don't talk about diet or weight unless it is a fitness group! Never talk about medical issues in a group; those things can be discussed with intimate friends or family. Lend assistance whenever you can; offer to let someone go ahead. Help the hostess pick up dishes after dinner, if you are at a friend's home. Bring a hostess gift. Enjoy being a charming heavenly woman! It is fun.

LIVING IT:

Listen to the sound of your voice this week. Are there times when you let it get strident or demanding? It's like the old saying: you draw more flies with honey than vinegar. Well, that doesn't sound like a very good analogy, does it? But you know what I mean. Suppose you're having a discussion with your mate. Saying things kindly and gently probably will be listened to more completely than if the tone was off-putting.

Set a pretty table with extra forks and spoons, napkins. If you have children or grandchildren, teach them how to use them.

FOR FUN:

Becoming more charming and pleasant can be easy and fun. Look at the chart on the next page and try to determine what styles are best for you. Circle anything on the whole chart that you think describes you, then you should find where most of the circles are, and that can indicate your style type according to your height, build, carriage, face shape, eyes, nose, mouth, hair, and coloring. Then look at the chart that shows prints and styles for the different types, and transfer what your type is to it. Sometimes it is helpful to have a friend do it with you for more objectivity. Make it a fun time!

Do an online search for images of a celebrity that is shaped sort of like you: (curvy or straight. Maybe ample or lean.) Find looks that you like, even though you would never have thought of wearing combinations like they do. Go through your closet and drawers to find things that you could mix for new looks.

Remember your best colors from our color chapter, and find your favorite of your best. Can you find ways to make it your signature color? Do you feel pretty in it? Charming?

YIN/YANG CHART TO DETERMINE WOMEN'S STYLE TYPES
Circle the boxes that nearest describe you,
then complete the Yin/Yang chart on the next page to determine your best style

	DRAMATIC	NATURAL	CLASSIC	ROMANTIC	GAMIN	INGENUE
Height	Above Average: 5'8" and up	Above average: 5'7" and up	Average: 5'6" or 5'7"	Average: 5'6" or 5'7"	Below Average: 5'3" to 5'5"	Below Average: 5'3" and below
Build	Fashion Figure: angular, long legs, may be thin.	Strong, muscular, squarish shoulders, may be stocky or pear-shaped	Well-proportioned; 6" wrist	Beautiful curves, may have long legs, ample bust	Small boned, less than 6" wrist, well proportioned, bouncy, lively	Small boned, dainty, appears frail, smaller than 6" wrist
Carriage	Erect, head held high, lively, sauntering	Relaxed, casual, vigorous, flat-heels, solid, outdoorsy	Poised, well balanced, erect, quiet repose, neat	Relaxed, willowy, soft, may be flirty	Alert, perky, hands on hips, athletic, pixie-like, girlish	Ballet posture, head tilted, graceful, appealing, innocent-like
Face Shape	Long oval, high cheekbones, angular, hollow cheeks, may be beautiful, unusual	Broad, long, or with square jaw; wide forehead, unusual	Oval; good cheekbones, pretty.	Very pretty, heart-shaped, triangular, beautiful	Rounded chin and cheeks, cute.	Round cheeks, round chin, or pointed little fairy face
Eyes	Deep set, heavy lid, closed, angled, slanted	Average size, friendly, approachable	Average size, clear direct gaze	Large, pretty, long lashes, alluring glance	Wide open, wide apart, large, twinkling, friendly	Large, round, wide open, long lashes, coy, demure
Nose	Long, pointed, or irregular shape, flared nostrils	Irregular, or heavy, blunt, large	Straight, well-shaped, average	Delicate, long, straight or turned up	Short, button, rounded, turned up	Dainty, fine, upward tilt
Mouth	Wide, flat curve, or heavy lips	Wide, average or heavy, smiling	Well-molded	Curvy, full lips, cupid's bow, dimples	Small, rounded, smiling, saucy	Rosebud or heart-shaped, soft, small
Hairstyle	Plain, severe, fashion extreme, chignon, any length	Casual, short and unset, mannish, or long, wavy, tousled	Simple, neat, plain, waves not tight curls. Usually shoulder length or shorter	Long, soft curls, below shoulders	Short, fluffy, natural; bangs or feathered, pony tail	Curly or straight, short or long, wears ballet bun well or pony tail
Coloring	Definite contrasts	Medium, rich, or light	Medium or light contrasts	Rich, radiant	Medium contrasts	Light, fair

Height	Face shape	Eyes	Nose	Mouth	Hairstyle	Coloring	PRINTS	CLOTHING STYLES
							Dramatic	Extreme high fashion, long draped clinging silhouette, angular or S-curve lines, unusual details, satin, heavy rich fabrics, great contrasts, extreme hats and accessories, diagonal lines, pointed or jagged prints, bold geometric.
							Natural	Rough textures, natural fabric finishes, raw silk, shantung, tweeds, bulky knits, lumpy fabrics; casual, comfortable; natural accessories like shells, wood beads, leather; no "cute" details like bows; any lace or ruffles should be natural or country; fairly pointed prints, geometric.
							Classic	Smart, simple, refined; no extreme fashions. Smooth fabrics, small geometric or pretty, neat prints. May be simplified romantic, gamin, or ingenue. Tasteful.
							Romantic	Softly feminine, draped bows, soft gathers, full skirts, fitted bodices, lace, chiffon, velvet; dainty jewelry and accessories. Lovely prints; no bold stripes or geometrics. Fitted jackets.
							Gamin	Fresh, All-American Girl look; pleated skirts, short jackets, gingham and plaids, peter pan collars, scallops, some riffles, narrow bows, eyelet lace, ric-rac, rounded prints, small object prints.
							Ingenue	Fragile, dainty, young look; gathered fullness, ruffles, organdy, voile, dotted swiss, soft angora, very rounded, tiny prints; fine stripes; cute jewelry and accessories. This look often matures into one of the other categories.

The Yin-Yang Charts to Determine Your Best Style

Chapter 17

THE STRESS-FREE WOMAN—
BANISHING ANXIETY
AND WORRY

A few years ago, I began to have stomach trouble. I, who had been able to eat anything I wanted to, and had never even needed a Tum. Now I couldn't eat the mildest thing without terrible indigestion, and the whole digestive tract was causing trouble from start to end. I asked for prayer and did a lot of praying about it myself, yet day and night I was miserable. Food felt like lead in my stomach, so I didn't eat much. I tried all the home remedies I could find, but finally went to my doctor to see what was going on. The specialist who did a scope to see what was going on said that my stomach had rebelled about something and developed severe chronic gastritis, which I was told took a long time getting to the place where I felt it, and the lining of my stomach was in really bad shape. I was put on medicine to stop any digestive acids forming in my stomach, and it was amazing how wonderful I felt immediately. I had no more pain, could eat anything, and slept through the nights. The doctor said I would be on the medicine for probably the rest of my life.

It felt good, but there was a cloud in the sunny sky: acid is necessary to digest minerals, especially calcium, and because of my fragile bones, this caused me concern. Something else to be anxious about, actually! I talked with my doctor about it, and he agreed that since my bones were so porous due to osteoporosis, we should look for alternatives to the medicine.

One day I happened to read that the brain and gut are connected by something called the vagus nerve, one of the largest nerves in the body. This nerve sends signals from the brain to gut and vice versa, increasing digestive irritability and irregularity when stress and anxiety occurs. I didn't think I was anxious, and my life seemed pretty stress-free. But I began to pray about it, and what the Lord showed me was a blow, but it rang true: *I was a worrier.*

As I looked back over my early life, I noticed that I was the *one* out of nine kids at home who seemed to make it my business to check out most situations to see if there was any danger. Yes, I could now see that I was an *anxious* kid. Anxious that someone might get hurt. Anxious that there would be ramifications of certain activity. Anxious that I wouldn't do well or that I would say the wrong thing and be thought ignorant. Anxious that I wouldn't remember what I needed to remember. Anxious about whatever came up. And I didn't even know it! I just thought I was the cautious one, making sure the "little kids" stayed far back from the edge of a cliff. I was the sensible one, when my 10-year-old sister Berta bravely walked a high horizontal tree branch, a dizzying 20 feet above a hard gravel driveway, while 8-year-old me scooted along it "sensibly" on my backside holding on for dear life. Anxiously.

I was young and vigorous, and all that worrying didn't affect my health—then. Reminds me of the people who smoke cigarettes when young and say, "It won't kill me for years." The body is resilient, and it does take years to break down. My wake-up call about worrying came when my stomach had had enough, so I started a real intentional study to find out what I needed to do.

Of course, it made sense to research what foods make stomach distress worse, and which ones aid healing, resulting in some drastic changes to my diet. It made some difference, but there was still quite a problem. I sensed God was showing me that a spiritual problem was at the root of it all. As I sought answers from the Bible, I was floored by the sheer number of scripture verses I found that dealt with anxiety, nervousness, worry, and fears! Look at a few:

> An anxious heart weighs a man down, but a kind word cheers him up (Proverbs 12:25 NIV).

There is so much in our world that weighs hearts down. It is no wonder that Omeprozole (the acid stopper for tummies) is on the top 10 list of prescribed drugs in America, having doubled in the last ten years! As heavenly women, we can, with practical answers and God's grace, banish anxiety in ourselves; and the above Proverb shows that we can relieve stress in others too by giving out kind words to cheer up those around us.

> So then, banish [forbid, abolish, or get rid of something unwanted] anxiety from your heart and cast off the troubles of your body, for youth and vigor are meaningless. (Ecclesiastes 11:10 NIV)

The last part of that verse is interesting. As I found out, when my body was young and vigorous, the stomach managed to hold its own, even though I was constantly anxious about something. But youth flees, and vigor slips away, and the stress catches up with you, so I think the verse in Ecclesiastes means "don't count on your youth and vigor, because they don't mean anything in this area long term."

> Do not be anxious about anything, but in everything, by prayer and petition, with thanksgiving, present

your requests to God. And the peace of God,
which transcends all understanding, will guard your
hearts and your minds in Christ Jesus. (Philippians
4:6-7 TLV)

When you catch anxiety sneaking into your situation,
remember that God doesn't say, "I hope you won't be anxious;"
but he does say, "DO NOT be anxious about anything." Being
a good Father, he has rules that we need to follow, if we want
a good, peaceful life, much like we have rules for our children.
We don't say, "I'd really like it if you didn't play on the highway,
because you could get hurt." We make it completely clear that
they DO NOT play on the highway; it is an enforced and strict
rule for their good. And just like the above Philippians verse says,
God promises he is available to help. Like with our children's DO
NOT PLAY IN THE HIGHWAY rule, we tell them that if they
need to cross the busy highway, they only need ask us and we
will safely take them across. A well-loved child will know we are
there to help, even in things they don't understand. When they are
more mature, they will be able to manage the busy highway, but
they need to submit to our wiser leadership while they are still
learners. Just like children, we need to accept humbly that God
loves us, and His mighty hand will lead us through difficulty and
in due time, "lift us up."

Humble yourselves, therefore, under God's mighty
hand, that he may lift you up in due time. Cast all
your anxiety on him because he cares for you. (1
Peter 5:6,7) (Also see Psalm 55:22-23 NIV)

What do we worry about? What we have to eat? Or not eat?
Or whether we have a budget that stretches around our bills? Do
we *know* that God loves us and that we are very valuable to Him?

Then Jesus said to his disciples: "Therefore I tell you, do not worry about your life, what you will eat; or about your body, what you will wear. Life is more than food, and the body more than clothes. Consider the ravens: They do not sow or reap, they have no storeroom or barn; yet God feeds them. And how much more valuable you are than birds! Who of you by worrying can add a single hour to his life? Since you cannot do this very little thing, why do you worry about the rest?" (Luke 12:22—26 NIV). (Also see Matthew 6:25—34)

We have lived in these bodies on this mortal earth for many years, and we have a natural propensity to worry, because in this life we are often let down, abandoned, rejected; and our body breaks down. But once we have come to Christ, and realize how valuable we are to Him, how He gave his very life for us, and how much our Heavenly Father wants to give us a peaceful life, it should be all different. We are to take our problems to the Father, and after we do so and still feel wobbly inside, we can actually speak to our own soul to "get up and quit worrying, hope in God, and you will in the end have reason to praise him":

Why my soul, are you downcast? Why so disturbed within me? Put your hope in God, for I will yet praise him, my Savior and my God. (Psalm 42:5 NIVUK).

We are sojourners of this life, learning to trust an unseen God. We are heavenly women, placed among busy families, piles of laundry, impossible schedules, husbands who think so differently than we do. It is hard to understand how it can all work out ok. But God says, don't worry about understanding it all, just lay it all out to Him, "acknowledge Him" (telling your soul that God will take care of it), and He promises to untangle your life. Learn His ways, leave behind the old worrying ways, and you will find the abundant life!

> Trust in the LORD with all your heart and lean
> not on your own understanding; in all your ways
> acknowledge him, and he will make your paths
> straight. Do not be wise in your own eyes; fear the
> LORD and shun evil. This will bring health to your
> body and nourishment to your bones. (Proverbs
> 3:5—8 NIV)

Sometimes in the midst of it all, we feel too exhausted to pray, too weak to stand up and be brave. How can we even know how to pray? Well, God has even thought of that. He said he would send His Holy Spirit to us to help our weakness and—amazement of amazement—He says the Holy Spirit will actually do the praying *for* us, because He knows exactly what the Will of God is for us and for all "the saints" (heavenly women and their families and associates)!

> The Spirit helps us in our weakness. We do not
> know what we ought to pray for, but the Spirit
> himself intercedes for us with groans that words
> cannot express. And he who searches our hearts
> knows the mind of the Spirit, because the Spirit
> intercedes for the saints in accordance with God's
> will. And we know that in all things God works for the
> good of those who love him, who have been called
> according to his purpose. (Romans 8:26—28 ESV)

> "And my God will meet all your needs according
> to his glorious riches in Christ Jesus." (Philippians
> 4:19 NIV)

> "I can do everything through him who gives me
> strength." (Philippians 4:13 NLT)

The apostle Paul found his strength in God, and he reminds us that:

I have been in prison frequently, been flogged severely, and been exposed to death again and again. Five times I received from the Jews the forty lashes minus one. Three times I was beaten with rods, once I was stoned, three times I was shipwrecked, I spent a night and a day in the open sea, I have been constantly on the move. I have been in danger from rivers, in danger from bandits, in danger from my own countrymen, in danger from Gentiles; in danger in the city, in danger in the country, in danger at sea; and in danger from false brothers. I have known hunger and thirst and have often gone without food; I have been cold and naked. Who is weak, and I do not feel weak? Who is led into sin, and I do not inwardly burn? If I must boast, I will boast of the things that show my weakness. I will not boast about myself, except about my weaknesses. [God] said to me, "My grace is sufficient for you, for my power is made perfect in weakness." Therefore I will boast all the more gladly about my weaknesses, so that Christ's power may rest on me. That is why, for Christ's sake, I delight in weaknesses, in insults, in hardships, in persecutions, in difficulties. For when I am weak, then I am strong. (2 Corinthians 11:23—12:10 NIV)

So we say with confidence, 'The Lord is my helper; I will not be afraid. What can man do to me?' (Hebrews 13:6 NIV)

We have the promise that God *will* give us the Holy Spirit if we just ask. It is a simple prayer, and if you want the power of the Holy Spirit in your life, all you have to do once you realize God loves you and His own dear Son Jesus went to his death for you, is ask. "Father, I'm not heavenly yet but I want to be, and I know you have promised to help me—please fill me with your

Holy Spirit now." Then thank Him for that promise and start expecting He will give you guidance and help. He will.

> If you then, being evil, know how to give good gifts to your children, how much more will your heavenly Father give the Holy Spirit to those who ask Him? (Luke 11:13 ESV)

> Put your hope in the LORD both now and forevermore. (Psalm 131:3 NIV)

Also, especially if you are trying to banish worry, take time to read the entire reassuring passage in your Bible: Psalm 139:1-23. What does it say to you?

> I sought the LORD, and he heard me, and delivered me from all my fears (Psalm 34:4 NIV).

As I did seek the Lord about my gastrointestinal problems, I felt that He heard me and through the gentle prompting of the Holy Spirit and the written words of the Bible, He has "delivered me from all my fears [and anxieties and worries]." Now I know that Christ is our healer, and there are many promises in the Word about healing. It is a wonderful subject and really warrants a whole different study, dealing with the healing God gives us. But in this case, I was sure God was digging deep to help me quit doing what was *causing* my illness. I have been shown how destructive worrying is to our bodies, and I now *see* it more, and recognize it when I start being anxious again. I also know that old habits die hard, so I have to keep an eye out for a relapse into anxiety and worry.

Mental health experts tell us that our mind forms "mental maps" that become second nature, paths we go down without even thinking about it. It is much like the road to your house— your brain has made a mental map so you don't even have to think about it, you just drive there. I had to proactively redraw my mental map that used to take me down the worry path; I actually put cards on my fridge saying "re-draw your mental map" and "look out for bridges out" and things like that, to help me recognize that I was prone to go the wrong direction about anxiety and worry. The Lord is good to tip me off when I start down that old blind alley, so I can "repent" (turn around and go the other way), and stay on the straight and narrow path that leads to God's ways. His ways are full of peace and joy.

> When anxiety was great within me, your consolation brought me joy. (Psalm 94:19 NIV)

God has an abundant, carefree life in mind for each of us, and he has hope and good works planned for us. He has answers for those who will seek Him.

> Now may our Lord Jesus Christ Himself, and our God and Father, who has loved us and given us everlasting consolation and good hope by grace, comfort your hearts and establish you in every good word and work. (2 Thess. 2:16,17 NKJV)

LIVING IT:

The possible causes of anxiety and fear are many: conflict, health problems, dangerous situations, death, unmet needs, spiritual problems, false beliefs, etc.

> "According to the Bible, there is nothing wrong with realistically acknowledging and trying to deal with the identifiable problems of life. To ignore danger is foolish and wrong. But it is also wrong, as well as unhealthy, to be immobilized by worry. Such worry must be committed in prayer to God, who

can release us from paralyzing fear or anxiety, and free us to deal realistically with the needs and welfare both of others and of ourselves." (Dr. Gary R. Collins, <u>Christian Counseling</u>, p. 66.)

Here are some general, PRACTICAL common sense suggestions for those weighed down with fear, anxiety or worry:

- POSSIBLE SIN IN YOUR LIFE—Sometimes fear and anxiety are the result of one's own sin and guilt. If you have committed a sin or done anything evil, your fear and anxiety is probably God and your own conscience trying to get your attention. You need to repent, confess your sin, seek God's forgiveness, and set it right.
- EAT WELL—We don't have to be fiercely rigid about health food, but we should try to eat balanced, healthy meals. Avoid the bad, try to find the good foods; and it's ok to enjoy a treat once in awhile too. Comfort food can help combat the tension.
- GET ENOUGH SLEEP—Humans generally need 8 or 9 hours of sleep per day. Sleep deprivation can increase anxiety. Get enough rest. If you cannot sleep, you may need to seek God's help and perhaps that of a physician.
- BE MORE REALISTIC—Many people are worried and anxious about events that will never actually happen to them. Research shows that the things we fear aren't what actually happen. Relax. Focus on today. Take life one day at a time.
- LISTEN to relaxing, soothing music. There is some great Christian music available that can help you focus on God and leave your fears and worries behind. It may also help to listen to good Christian speakers and teachers.
- TALK to someone. Don't hold all the anxiety inside. It can be a big relief to share your fears and worries with

someone else who is qualified to understand and help—a pastor or counselor. If fear and anxiety is an ongoing problem in your life, schedule a regular time each week to talk with someone. Don't choose a friend or relative though—they might steer you in the wrong direction, if they are not trained in counseling.

- TAKE ACTION—If there is something practical and wise that you can do to alleviate the problem or avoid needless danger, take action. Don't put it off. Procrastination will generally raise your anxiety level.
- EXERCISE—Medical studies show that exercise can help lower anxiety. If you are healthy enough to exercise, try it. Regular brisk walks, running, swimming or other exercises can be a real stress reducer. Experts say if you enjoy an activity, it will be the one that will help you relieve stress, so think about activities that appeal to you.

FOR FUN:

If at all possible this week, do something that you enjoy. It is good to get some recreation on a regular basis. Make time THIS WEEK to do this.

Take a break. Get your mind off your fears and worries, and have some fun. Invite your spouse or call a friend and invite them for a cup of tea or something—not to dump your cares on them, but to enjoy them as a person. Go to a movie. Take a drive to see a beautiful view. Eat ice cream.

Chapter 18

THE FEARLESS WOMAN—
FACING THE ANCIENT FOE

We are heavenly women—seeking to be whole and free, but sometimes hindered by negative experiences in this world. As Vance Havner so correctly observes, "If you are a Christian, you are not a citizen of this world trying to get to heaven; you are a citizen of heaven making your way through this world."

Sarah, Abraham's beautiful wife, didn't start out being a heavenly woman. You will recall that when God told Abraham that Sarah would give him a son, she snickered and didn't believe. But her journey in faith, which took her many scary places, somehow brought her through. The New Testament testifies that not only did she learn to "obey" Abraham, she called him lord. Webster says lord means having authority over others, and it says "obsolete: husband, male head of household." Sadly, this current feminist culture says it is obsolete that there should be a male head of household, but in all the centuries up until this current generation, it was the familial order. This is not to say the husband is perfect or even everything a wife would prefer; but somehow, in God's design, the husband is assigned a position of authority (and corresponding responsibility). The Biblical view is that Christ is head of the husband, and that the husband is head of

205

the wife. Christ does not demand that a man follow Him, He just lays down His life for him out of love, and the man who accepts His love follows Him willingly with reciprocal love. Likewise, the husband also does not demand that a woman follow him, but lays his own independent life down for her, and she willingly follows him out of love and devotion, and they become "one."

> But I want you to understand that Christ is the head of every man, and the man is the head of a woman, and God is the head of Christ. (1 Corinthians 11:3 NASB)

Sarah had been through really hard times with Abraham, and had some trust issues. He actually lied to the king of Egypt (twice), resulting in Sarah ending up in the King's harem. Talk about scary! But she had learned that God was working in Abraham's life and that God had given Abraham fantastic promises; she had learned to trust God, and therefore could trust Abraham. Judith Cantrell wrote this: "It's better to listen to God than to listen to fear. Fear will defeat you. God will give you the win."

> ...just as Sarah obeyed Abraham, calling him lord, and you have become her children if you do what is right without being frightened by any fear. (1 Peter 3:6 NASB)

When I married Thomas, he perceived that I was fearful about many things. The fears interfered with my peace of mind. One of the first scripture verses he recited to me was:

> For God hath not given us the spirit of fear; but of power, and of love, and of a sound mind. (2 Timothy 1:7 KJV)

Fears. I know them—well. I'll share a few.
I have always hated saws. Everything from a little coping saw

to a chainsaw could bring unreasonable pictures flashing through my mind. Simple little circular saws might slip off the penciled line on the board and—I don't know what—but *be careful!* Band saws have yards of exposed teeth—*oh, do be careful!* I would try not to even think what damage could happen if you were using a chainsaw and tripped over a branch on the ground.

My dad had a sawmill with an exposed blade the size of a Volkswagen that my oldest son helped run, and I couldn't even watch him work. Although I was a builder's daughter, I never learned how to work with wood because of the fears I harbored about saws.

Saws weren't all I feared. Traffic paralyzed me to a point that I would make excuses to stay home rather than face the terror I felt with every imagined head-on crash. When I had to be a passenger, I made sure I had a book or magazine to read to get my eyes off the oncoming truck, bus, car or even curb. They were all out to get me.

And heights—the fear of falling made my knees go weak and my feet tingle and my head dizzy so I avoided climbing trees as a child. Even as an adult I couldn't bear to be near a cliff, and when on vacations with children at beautiful mountainous spots, I was petrified that one of the children would fall over a precipice.

Sensible caution is a good thing, but unreasonable fears had taken hold down deep in my being. Thomas recognized that something was not right. He shared the fear scripture with me and began to help me see how fear had been shaping my life. He prayed for me a lot, and God answered his prayer: my eyes were opened, and I realized the severity of the problem. I began to make it a matter of personal prayer to journey out of fear, and I have gotten the victory. However, I still, like an alcoholic, have to be vigilant against my old foe, fear.

How did fear get such a grip on me? Satan doesn't play fair. Like a lion who pulls down the weakest antelope of the fleeing herd, he picks on the weak, the young. What a bully!

> Keep a cool head. Stay alert. The Devil is poised
> to pounce, and would like nothing better than to
> catch you napping. Keep your guard up. You're
> not the only ones plunged into these hard times.
> It's the same with Christians all over the world. So
> keep a firm grip on the faith. The suffering won't last
> forever. It won't be long before this generous God
> who has great plans for us in Christ—eternal and
> glorious plans they are!—will have you put together
> and on your feet for good. He gets the last word;
> yes, he does. (1 Peter 5:8, MSG)

I want to share some of my experiences as I learned to overcome fear. As I sought the Lord about all this fear, He brought visions of the past before me. When I was about two, my dad was building a new home for us. The basement was finished and its cement floor poured. The "deck" (the builder's term for the main level floor) was on, and it was a beautiful expanse of smooth wooden floor, a perfect place for little girls to ride little tricycles—except for the opening in the floor deck left for the as yet un-built stairway to the basement below. The terror I must have felt as I rode over that edge and plunged to the basement floor below must have been matched by what my parents felt as they helplessly watched me disappear down that stairway hole. Mom told me years later as she had looked down at my motionless body, face down on the rock-hard cement floor with my little dress over my head and my diaper-end up, she thought I was dead. Did fear of heights and fear of falling enter my brain then? I don't know, but I suspect that moments of terror are entry points the ancient foe uses. As I began to pray about fear, the Lord brought that to mind, and I was able to dig out a root of fear.

As I tackled my unreasonable traffic fear, the Lord showed me a flashback of when I was 16. I had just gotten my learner's driving permit, and we were on a vacation in Arizona. One beautiful place we visited was at the top of a plateau overlooking a desert valley. As we stood taking pictures, we could see that the road descending was winding and steep. I was already frightened by being so close to the edge when my dad decided that I should drive us down. I was panicking, but he insisted, saying if I could drive that descent, I would be able to drive anywhere. He must have had nerves of steel, but I didn't. I felt like I died a thousand deaths by the time we reached the valley floor, and I never liked driving since! Seeing the root of the fear helped, but I had to actively fight that old foe every time I felt the fear arise. When I was a passenger and felt the panic and found my hands grabbing the dash and my feet bracing for an imagined crash, I would say, under my breath, "Satan, get behind me," and I would speak God's word, "God has not given me a spirit of fear." Each time I did this, it pushed out the panic! It truly was a miracle. Little by little, I gained normalcy in traffic, but it took a consistent fight against that spirit of fear. After a while, I realized I was enjoying going places with no thoughts of death or crashes! I have to be vigilant though, because once in a while I am enjoying a nice drive with hubby when a knife of fear unexpectedly cuts the joy. I recognize where it comes from and immediately reject it, and—poof—it is gone! The devil does keep trying, but he has no power against us when we submit ourselves to God and push back.

> Submit yourselves therefore to God. Resist the devil, and he will flee from you. (James 4:7 NKJV)

> God is strong, and he wants you strong. So take everything the Master has set out for you, well-made weapons of the best materials. And put them to use so you will be able to stand up to everything the Devil throws your way. This is no afternoon athletic contest that we'll walk away from and forget about in a couple of hours. This is for keeps, a life-or-death fight to the finish against the Devil and all his angels. (Ephesians 6:10—12 MSG)

It is all too easy to forget that we are in a spiritual battle here on earth—but we are! Once our eyes are opened to this, we are no longer deceived, and we know the key! St. Peter, the first leader of the Christian church, was given the keys to the spirit world:

> Simon Peter answered, "You are the Messiah, the Son of the living God." Jesus answered "I will give you the keys of the kingdom of heaven; whatever you bind on earth will be bound in heaven, and whatever you loose on earth will be loosed in heaven." (Matthew 16:16—19, MSG)

Peter, a man full of fear and doubts and denial, just like us, was chosen to lead the way in establishing the Church on earth after Jesus was taken up again to heaven. *We* are the Church, the Body of Christ here on earth. *We* have the keys. *We* can bind Satan, who is running around creating havoc in our lives, our marriages, our homes, everywhere he can find a little crack to slip in. We have to remind ourselves that we are at war. *We* are God's army, doing battle for our loved ones, binding Satan and praying for deliverance for those around us. We are Heavenly Women, we are the Joan of Arcs in our day. We need to open our eyes to see that we are victors over Satan.

Todd Bentley wrote about the supernatural world around us, and says "Gehazi, Elisha's servant, was fearful because he *saw* only with his natural eyes. Elisha *saw* into the *spiritual realm* with his spiritual eyes. He *saw* the real world." Read about the servant's eyes being opened to the spirit battle all around them:

> One time when the king of Aram was at war with Israel, after consulting with his officers, he said, "At such and such a place I want an ambush set."
> The Holy Man sent a message to the king of Israel: "Watch out when you're passing this place, because Aram has set an ambush there."

So the king of Israel sent word concerning the place of which the Holy Man had warned him.

This kind of thing happened all the time.

The king of Aram was furious over all this. He called his officers together and said, "Tell me, who is leaking information to the king of Israel? Who is the spy in our ranks?"

But one of his men said, "No, my master, dear king. It's not any of us. It's Elisha the prophet in Israel. He tells the king of Israel everything you say, even what you whisper in your bedroom."

The king said, "Go and find out where he is. I'll send someone and capture him."

The report came back, "He's in Dothan."

Then he dispatched horses and chariots, an impressive fighting force. They came by night and surrounded the city.

Early in the morning a servant of the Holy Man got up and went out. Surprise! Horses and chariots surrounding the city! The young man exclaimed, "Oh, master! What shall we do?"

He said, "Don't worry about it—there are more on our side than on their side."

Then Elisha prayed, "O GOD, open his eyes and let him see."

The eyes of the young man were opened and he saw. A wonder! The whole mountainside full of horses and chariots of fire surrounding Elisha! (2 Kings 6:8—23 MSG)

Back to my fears. Saws—still a problem. I had let that fear lie dormant because my dad is gone, as is his dreaded sawmill, and Thomas is not into carpentry. But now my young grandson has picked up my dad's mantle, so to speak. He has a *sawmill*. Smaller, with a protected blade, he assures me. Oh, BE CAREFUL! He also cuts delicate little items out of wood with a band saw, that dreaded thing with yards of teeth. *Do be careful!* So, I have had to face this old foe who has hidden for 60 some years. As I prayed for understanding, a day came back to me: as a four-old, I was playing in Daddy's wood shop. He was using the table saw, and he must have been a most unusually patient (if perhaps not careful) daddy to allow me to play in the sawdust around his feet as he worked. I remember seeing how the sawdust sifted down under the underside of the rotating saw, a steady stream of soft sawdust, making a heap like snow. I reached my little left hand into the table saw's lower chamber to touch the sawdust, and the next thing I knew there was blood flying and I screamed and Daddy grabbed me up and ran to the house. Mom wound a kitchen towel around my hand and I remember her holding it tight as Daddy drove us furiously to the doctor's, and then I remember the doctor binding it up and saying that it would be ok and someday maybe they could operate to straighten the nail. (I still have a twisted end and bent nail on my shortened ring finger, which has always saddened me.) So, it wasn't as bad as they had first thought, but in my mind, it was pure horror. The SAW was my enemy from then on, a deceptive monster. But now the real enemy is exposed: when the fear rises up, I deal with it the same as I have learned to deal with the other fears: resist the devil and speak God's truth—and the fear has to go. It really works!

As we press on toward becoming heavenly women, we see things in our lives that hold us back. For me, fear was one of those. It was interfering with my peace, and was a problem that caused difficulties in relationships. It caused trouble with my husband because I couldn't bear for him to use a chainsaw, which can be so necessary in keeping extensive grounds in check. It rendered me useless in emergencies because if anyone got hurt, my grown kids would say, "Don't tell Mom, she would freak out." God has an answer for us, and if we are serious about leaving our weaknesses behind and moving into a better future, He will help us.

But one thing I do: Forgetting what is behind and straining toward what is ahead, I press on toward the goal to win the prize for which God has called me. (Philippians 3:12—17 NIV)

LIVING IT:

Look at your life and ask God to show you if there is an area of your life that holds you back from being all you could be. Are there fears that have taken hold somewhere along your life? Maybe it isn't things like fear of heights or saws; it may be a hidden fear of trusting God, unsure if He will really come through for you. For instance, if your relationship with your father caused negative trust issues, you might be fearful of trusting men, even your husband. See if you can, like Sarah, learn to trust God to manage the situation, and begin to obey Him and bring glory to your situation by being a heavenly woman, not afraid to be vulnerable and trusting of others. If God shows you something, ask Him for guidance and help in dealing with it. Remember the Sarah verse about submitting to God and not being afraid of any fear.

FOR FUN:

Find a photo snapped of a happy moment in your childhood or early marriage and put it out to enjoy. Perhaps frame it. If you can find only neutral photos, look at them with positive possibility thoughts. For instance, I have a photo of Mom holding me as a baby wrapped in a blanket. Mom doesn't look either happy or sad, but as a mom myself, I can imagine her thinking what a sweet bundle she was holding: her own healthy baby girl that had fine, peach-fuzz hair (I still do). Build memories of the good moments, as you conquer the negative ones. For some reason, bad moments seem to have their hooks in our brains, but as we deal with them, let us also replace them with good thoughts. Remember this great verse and apply it to all areas of your life:

> Finally, brothers and sisters, whatever is true, whatever is noble, whatever is right, whatever is pure, whatever is lovely, whatever is admirable—if anything is excellent or praiseworthy—think about such things. (Philippians 4:8 NIV)

Chapter 19

THE MATURE WOMAN— EMBRACING HER AUTUMN

There is a time to mourn and a time to dance!
Ecclesiastes 3:4

"Age gracefully," said my mom. Her hair was naturally a dark brown, and she helped it stay rich and dark when it started to gray; but I remember her saying that women should stop covering gray at 70. However, she did accent her brownish gray with some silver highlights! I guess she thought that just because we get older, we don't have to be dull. Many women embrace their gray hair, especially if they wear cool colors. If you wear warm colors better than cool colors, you could accent your gray with blond highlights instead of silver. I hear that blondes have more fun, so I thought, "Why not embrace my gray in a way that is fun?"

There comes a day when you glance at yourself reflected in the window of a shop and see an old lady. It is a shock. One year, when Mom got her new driver's license, she told me they put the picture of an old woman on it; that was her moment of truth. We do grieve when the reality hits us, and maybe we just have a good private cry. But then we need to shake ourselves and say, "This is the day that the Lord has made. We will rejoice and be glad in it." We need to quit looking back, and instead look for the good that we have, and what wonders lie ahead. As Robert Burns put it: "Grow old along with me, for the best is yet to be." The Apostle Paul reminds us that even as our body ages, our spirit is alive and growing each day:

> Therefore we do not lose heart. Though outwardly we are wasting away, yet inwardly we are being renewed day by day. (2 Cor 4:16 NIV)

> Forgetting the past, we press on.... (Philippians 3:12 KJV)

Accept your limitations. If you are older now, you can't do everything you used to. The great thing is that you actually don't *want* to do everything you used to do. I remember that when our children were small, we would take them to the river where we swam all day and evening, hating to have to gather up the picnic things and head for home as dusk fell. Now when I see my grown kids planning huge picnic outings, I'm more than glad to not go. I just don't have the stamina for the long exhausting hours in the baking sun, so I actually want to stay home and enjoy a good book with peace and quiet. Been there, done that. Don't want to anymore.

OK, admit too that you can't wear everything you used to. But you don't have to! You don't have to keep up with any weird fashions or do anything you don't want to do. In my pre-Christian days, in the 60s, I wore miniskirts, bellbottom trousers that were such hip huggers that they looked like they might slip off the hips, long "fall" wigs, false eyelashes, halter tops, hot pants, and who knows what else—and back then I then wouldn't be caught dead in "old lady" styles. Now I prefer sensible and beautiful clothing, and I couldn't care less what odd things the current young people wear, nor what they think of what I wear. When we are maturing, we can finally just dress and do as we prefer. We can smile, knowing that we have the last laugh, because the young people think they will always be young and smooth-skinned and full of energy; but we know the truth that they will someday learn too.

It is well and good to laugh and enjoy our just desserts about the privileges of mature age, but along with the fun parts of aging comes the realization that our bodies are a fragile ecosystem that we dare not abuse or be careless about. As we start to see parts of our bodies break down, we do get serious about health. Lose the pounds. Get moving. Cut out (or down) sugar and desserts. Taste it, enjoy it—like Gwen Shamblin, author of an amazing diet book, THE WEIGH DOWN DIET, who can enjoy an m&m thoroughly. One. She also delights in a lovely, golden, crisp, salty potato chip. One. The old TV ad we heard back in the day was "Nobody eats just one!" It must have been brilliant ad copy, because after many years I can still hear that jingle in my head! But it's not true. We *can* eat just one, and with real appreciation, thoroughly enjoy it, while not abusing our poor little physical body. When we get serious about wanting to enjoy our older years and treat our bodies carefully, we can enjoy the taste, not the waste (or the waist!).

Enjoy each day. You realize you don't have unlimited days now. When I was young, I never gave it a thought. "I'll do that someday," I would think, about activities or dreams. "Someday I would like to live in a cottage by the sea," or "Someday maybe we can have an apartment in London and a home in the US, and spend months back and forth." Someday was a long, beautifully vague idea, with lots and lots of possibilities and room in it. When you are maturing, and as you browse the garden catalog, you say, "let's plant a pecan tree in the garden." Then suddenly you realize that in all likelihood you would never see a pecan from it. You just don't have the time left. So time becomes valuable and precious.

Youth wastes time because it feels immortal. (Well, as Christians, we are immortal, in a sense, but I'm talking about our time on earth.) I say they waste time, but I guess I really mean they don't value it, because it seems to be limitless.

When I was young, I was in good health and could do anything I wanted to. I could ice skate, climb hills, run several miles, swim, even do flips off the diving board. Had I been told that someday I would no longer be able to run, and that hiking up my hill would be out of the question, I wouldn't have believed it. I sort of thought when I was young and "immortal," that because I looked after my diet and exercised and was a "clean-living person," I wouldn't age like the elderly people I saw. I guess I thought they must have not taken care of themselves. Well, wisdom comes with age: we do wear out. No matter how robust and active my parents were, they did actually wear out and pass away. I will too. To every person there is appointed time. Live with it, embrace it, enjoy the allotted days. They are precious.

I have always thought that as we age, we get either bitter or better. It is up to us. As Christian women, we should surely get better, as we have God on our side to help us. You do see a lot of bitter old people, and I have asked God to help me to never end up that way. I have always wanted to become a heavenly woman, and now I have added a word: I want to eventually become a heavenly *old* woman.

I have a little book entitled, YOU DON'T HAVE TO BE OLD WHEN YOU GROW OLD, by Florence Tompkins Taylor, which tells a memorable and heartwarming story. The author tells about having to give up her own home when she could no longer take care of it, and she reluctantly moved in with her son's family. It was a large happy group who loved her and welcomed her. However, she felt sad and sorry for herself. All of her well-loved furniture had been sold or given away, and all she had was what could fit in the little spare room that was supposed to be her home now. One afternoon, as she lay on the bed trying to take a nap, there was quite a ruckus in the yard below. The grandchildren were playing, as children do, merrily and noisily on the lawn, a game of softball. She thought they might have some consideration for an old lady trying to nap, but if anything, the noise just increased. As she lay there feeling quite annoyed at the noise, and somewhat bitter about no longer having her own home, she complained to the Lord. She tells of hearing God speak plainly to her: "Perhaps you would rather be in a nice, quiet nursing home?" When God speaks, you listen! She immediately saw how ungrateful she had been, and repented and asked for forgiveness. Just then there was a loud crash of splintering glass, and a softball and pieces of glass landed on her bed! Then silence below. Then thundering little footsteps on the stairs as the troupe of mini ballplayers rushed upstairs and burst open her door, horrified, saying, "Grandma, are you OK?" Since God had just visited her, she was a changed woman, able to burst out laughing, putting them at ease, just glad to be there among her people who loved her and cared about her.

Sometimes older people start following the Lord after wasted years and are so regretful they feel deep sadness and look backwards with negative feelings. They see how they missed so many things, and even how their mistakes caused problems in the lives of their children in many ways. While it is a good thing to take responsibility for our wrongs, it does nobody any good to dwell on regrets. There is a great way to get out of the weeds and into the sunshine and flowers of happy maturity: you see your past sins and apologize to anyone you have hurt. You have a complete change of heart, telling God how sorry you are, and He is ready and willing to—get this—completely erase them from your account! So then let them go!

> If we confess our sins, He is faithful and just to forgive us our sins and to cleanse us from all unrighteousness. (1 John 1:9. KJV)

> Create in me a clean heart, O God, and renew a steadfast spirit within me. Psalm 51:10. (KJV)

The LORD is compassionate and gracious, slow to anger, abounding in love. He does not treat us as our sins deserve or repay us according to our iniquities. As far as the east is from the west, so far has he removed our transgressions from us. (Psalm 103:8 NIV)

To every thing there is a season,
and a time to every purpose under the heaven:
A time to be born, a time to die;
a time to plant, and a time to pluck up that which is planted;
A time to kill, and a time to heal;
a time to break down, and a time to build up;
A time to weep, and a time to laugh;
a time to mourn, and a time to dance;
A time to cast away stones, and a time to gather stones together;
a time to embrace, and a time to refrain from embracing;
A time to get, and a time to lose;
a time to keep, and a time to cast away;
A time to rend, and a time to sew;
a time to keep silence, and a time to speak;
A time to love, and a time to hate;
A time of war, and a time of peace. (Ecclesiastes 3:1—8 KJV)

One of the surprises of mature life is about love. As we studied earlier, there are four different words for love in the Greek Bible, all translated into the English "love." But the four words show a growth of the quality of love that you can't fathom as a young lover. Early marriage has its intoxicating "eros" romantic love that brings two people together to unite and make a new family unit. It is all-consuming and fiery. As the years go by, eros is given a nice comfortable cushion to live on, the "storge" love, a comforting, homey love. While still very much enjoying romantic love, the partners have built a home life where they feel content and grounded together along with their children. These are very busy years, but the children do grow up, and finally the partners have time to be best friends, to do things together, just the two of them. So the heady "eros" love, bound in a family unit "storge" love with its memories and traditions, becomes interwoven with "phileo" love, the friendship love. Then it gets even better: in older years, as time becomes more precious and the partners have twined together in their spiritual lives, the unselfish "agape," the best most Godly love of all, becomes most prominent. The other three loves take a back seat. Physical "eros" love is less and less a part of the mix. As the kids grow up and have their own lives, the family "storge" love traditions and family times—at least the ones we host—grow fewer. What is left may seem to young onlookers to be two old people who don't know about love anymore; but the older couple can smile knowingly at each other, because we oldies have known all four kinds of love, and they are crowned by the best love of all, "agape," the heavenly type of love.

All our lives most of us have scrimped to buy our kids shoes or milk and to keep a roof over their heads, and we tried to save for a rainy day or for our old age. Well, some of us are *in* our old age, so it's OK for us to break open the old piggy bank and get a few pretty things for ourselves. It's fun to be older. I've seen some nasty outcomes of grown children fighting over the property or money that their old parents left when they passed away, and I wondered if the parents did them a favor by doing without so there would be something left for the children. The parents earned it, and they had every right to enjoy the fruits of their own labor! I saw a sign on a large and probably expensive motor home once that said, "We are spending our children's inheritance." And they looked like they were having the time of their lives. It can be fun to be older.

Admittedly though, with age comes trials too, usually physical problems. Thomas was always very fit and strong. In his younger years, he could outwork younger men when it came to lifting heavy objects or working hard. Even in his early seventies, he was strong and worked lovingly in his garden and enjoyed keeping our grounds beautiful. There were a few falls when he lost his balance, but nothing serious: just age.

Then there came a day when he lost his footing when outside feeding his dog, "Bob." I was putting the finishing touches on supper, and he said he would take care of Bob and be back in a minute. Five minutes turned into ten, and I started to wonder what was keeping him. Just then he came into the kitchen, with lots of blood running down his face and onto his clothes. Startled, I asked, "What happened? Did you fall?" He seemed a bit confused, and said, "No, why?" He had no memory of falling or getting up and was oblivious to all the blood. I started to mop the blood with a paper towel and discovered a terrible gash on his forehead! I dropped everything and took him to the emergency room, where it was determined that he had a "brain bleed," and was transferred to a larger city hospital and admitted. It was during the COVID-19 panic of 2020, and I was not allowed to go with him, or even enter the hospital at all. It was a traumatizing time for him, because he had become quite hard of hearing and depended on my helping him understand what was being said, so he had no idea what was happening to him. And it was a trying time for me because I so wanted to be with him, to comfort him and look out for him.

After two weeks he was able to come home, but things were different. He was supposed to use a walker because he was unsteady on his feet, and he was having trouble remembering things. His responses were not good when he was in traffic, and after some close calls, we agreed that I would do any driving. It seemed that his body was wearing out all at once. He had to have a toe amputated and had several skin cancers removed. He would get out of breath when he worked in the flower gardens, and had so little breath that he could hardly speak until he had rested awhile. His beautiful singing voice seemed to disappear, and he was so sad about that. That year was our biggest trial, as I entered a new phase of being his nurse as well as sweetheart. It was not a burden for me, because I found that our love had grown so much over the years that I wanted to be the one to be there for him, and to dress his wounds and take him to specialists. But it was a whole new thing. He didn't like being dependent on me; he was used to taking care of *me*. He didn't like not being able to do all the things he used to.

He did recover enough after a while to be back in his garden; he recovered from the skin cancers and seemed to be getting his breath back somewhat. We were happy to be through with the hard stuff, put that bad year behind us, and look forward to finally enjoying our retirement.

Then we both got bad colds. His was worse—so much so that I took him to the doctor, and was shocked when tests said he had COVID-19, the deadly early Delta variant. The next day they tested me, and I tested positive too. We both became so ill that my daughter came to stay with us and nearly wore herself out running between two sick parents. We couldn't keep any food or liquid down, and our lungs were so congested that our oxygen levels kept dipping very low. We both ended up in the hospital. He was in ICU, but I was released to recover at home because I was a bit less ill, and the hospital was full. I was still too sick to visit him, and none of the family could visit him because of the COVID restrictions. But after a couple of weeks, I was able to go sit with him a little while each afternoon or evening and try to get him to eat a little. He was moved from ICU to a private room, but still he was too ill to be released. Then they moved him back to ICU, because they said he needed more oxygen.

One morning I awoke early and was reading the Bible. I came to Ecclesiastes 3:2, "There is a time to be born and a time to die." It seemed almost in bold print to me, as though it was an urgent message. I cried out to God, "Surely you aren't saying that

Thomas will die today?" Then almost immediately my son called and said, "Why don't I take you in to see Dad this morning?" (I had been going in the afternoon and evenings, but somehow he had just felt that we should go early in the morning.) So we went, and as I began to enter Thomas's ICU room, the doctor was right there, and asked me to step into the hall. The news was that Thomas was much worse, and in fact, they needed to put him on a ventilator immediately. The doctor said it was his only chance, and even then he might not make it, so if there was any family that might want to come say goodbye, I should contact them. I was shocked, even though in my Bible reading, the thought had occurred to me. My son and I went into the Thomas's room and told him what the doctor needed to do. It was a scary time for us both, and I hugged him and we said some sad goodbyes before they sedated him; we knew if the vent was successful, we would see each other when he woke up. But if it was not successful—we agreed that we would see each other in heaven. We were so sad, frightened, but peaceful.

Several hours later, the doctor came to us in the ICU waiting room with shocking news. Thomas's lungs were so destroyed by COVID that they were just torn apart when they tried to use the ventilator, and he didn't make it. The reality of it overwhelmed me, and of course I cried and cried. My faithful partner, my other half, my friend—was never coming back! The doctor said that his lungs were so bad that even if he had somehow pulled through, he would never be off oxygen, and his life would be one of an invalid. My son and I agreed that even though losing him was terrible, he would not have wanted that kind of life. At least he was able to live the life he loved up until the last month.

It has been a year and a half now since I lost him. There has been time to count the precious experiences we had together, and I have learned to look for the good. Instead of dwelling on him being gone, I rejoice in what we had. It was a long journey for me, from the very young and naïve woman who had so much to learn about being a wife, to the older woman who somehow was blessed with a man who adored her more and more each year, up until the fullness of time for us as a couple.

At first, widowhood made my life feel so turned upside down. I had been a pastor's wife for about as long as I could remember, and my identity was so wrapped up in his profession that it took a while for me to feel normal alone. But God has been so real to me and has helped me, step by step. I am learning to enjoy this new stage in life—widowhood—and take more time with grandchildren, more time to pursue my art, time to repaint my rooms according to my feminine tastes. I am able to enjoy things that I didn't for years; for instance, I have traveled with my daughter for a week at St. Petersburg beach in Florida. Actually, she was surprised when she learned that I loved the beach. Because Thomas did not swim, all she remembered was that we didn't ever go to the beach. Another thing I just experienced was an amazing trip when one of my sons took me to Hawaii, a place I never had visited because when Thomas and I traveled we always went the other direction to visit his family in England. I loved England, but now I can enjoy other places. As God showed me, "There is a season for everything under the sun; a time to be born, and a time to die." I must live in the season I'm in and not pine for the one that has passed. I was blessed with a great adventure and a great love; but that was then. Now I embrace this new time that God has given me.

If you are a "mature woman," perhaps a widow, this is *your* time. Yours alone, literally. Don't let the past be a tearful reminder of what you have lost; instead, let the past bring you joyful memories of the blessings, the good times. Be grateful for what you got to experience. Even the part of you that so misses the man you loved can say, "It is better to have loved and lost, than never loved at all." It is so true.

One of the first gifts Thomas gave me when we met was a cassette tape of him singing a song that said, "Yesterday is gone,

and tomorrow may never come, but we have this moment today."
I think I surmised when I listened to it that we would have great
moments together, but we cherished them "in the moment," and
I have no regrets. Bill Gaither wrote it. We played that beautiful
tape of Thomas singing it at his funeral!

Your Now is what you have. Enjoy it for its unique gifts. Take
God's hand and go with Him.

LIVING IT:

Get all those things out of the cupboards and closets that you
don't use because they are so good that you are saving them for
a special occasion. Now, don't panic! This isn't a time to get rid
of things and clear out closets. These are beloved things you
have saved up—this is your time to *enjoy* them! Here's the fun
part: now you get to *use* them. Burn that beautiful candle. Use
the perfume and lotion that were given to you in those beautiful
bottles that you have decorated your bathroom with for years.
Eat on china and use silverware and glassware. Use the nicest
place mats and napkins. Get those dresses out and wear them.

You are still you, and you deserve to look the part of God's
daughter. The pretty blouse that is "too pretty for daily wear" and
those cute sandals—they are for you, *now*. If you are at leisure
at home, don't just wear sweats or jeans and t-shirts. Put pretty
things on, wear makeup, do your hair. Put on your jewelry. After
all, at a mature age, you probably aren't going to be out hiking
on your hill or digging up a new garden every day if at all. You
might be enjoying your living room, and you might as well look
lovely in it. You have earned the right to be a lady of leisure! Be
a heavenly one!

When your grown kids come to visit, they can enjoy a happy, contented, fulfilled heavenly woman, and it will be cheerful. You can inspire them and give them hope that older years are not sad, sorry times to dread. Life can be beautiful. Embrace each phase of life. Be thankful to our merciful Father, who has been with us through it all, and takes our hand as we enjoy walking along the path of the rest of our journey.

FOR FUN:

Three times this week, dress nicely, even if you are just alone: well-groomed hair, makeup, jewelry, cute shoes—uniquely in your own style. Enjoy being who God designed you to be. Write a letter on pretty paper or a beautiful card and send it to a grandchild or other younger person. Reach across the ages and share the beauty.

> "Grow old along with me! The best is yet to be, the last of life, for which the first was made. Our times are in his hand who saith, 'A whole I planned, youth shows but half'; Trust God: See all, nor be afraid!" --Robert Browning

So, the journey I have been on is now closer to the end than the beginning, and it has been a path through the rose-filled spring, the sunshine and storms of summer, the gold and crimson glory of autumn, and the moonlit deep snows of winter, each a season of learning to walk in the ways of God's grace. I aim toward continuing to become a heavenly woman as much as possible here on earth, and finally, because of Christ, I *will* be a heavenly woman, forever. I am enjoying this fair path through life, and I encourage you too to press on, and follow the stepping stones through the beautiful garden of Christian womanhood.

CITATIONS

Chapter 1
Hannah Whitall Smith, *The Christian's Secret of a Happy Life,* (Revell, 2012)
Carole Jackson, *Color Me Beautiful,* (New York: Acropolis Books, 1980)

Chapter 2
Esther Burroughs, *Splash the Living Water; Turning Daily Interruptions into Life-giving Encounters* (Thomas Nelson, 1999)
Marie Kondo, *The Life-changing Magic of Tidying Up,* (KonMari Media, Inc., 2023)

Chapter 3
Marabel Morgan, *The Total Woman,* (Fleming H. Revell Company, 1973)
Edith Schaeffer, *The Hidden Art of Homemaking,* (Tyndale House Publishers, 1985)
Marie Kondo, *The Life-changing Magic of Tidying Up,* (KonMari Media, Inc., 2023)

Chapter 4
Larry Christensen, *The Christian Family,* (Bethany House Publishers, 1970)
Carole Jackson, *Color Me Beautiful,* (New York: Acropolis Books, 1980)

Chapter 5
Charles Dickens, *David Copperfield,* (Signet Classics, 2006)
Helen Andelin, *Fascinating Womanhood,* (Santa Barbara, Pacific Press 1969)

Chapter 6
Reinhold Niebuhr, *The Serenity Prayer*

Chapter 8
Andrea Burke, *The One Life Dream That Makes a Girl Blush,* (Rochester, NY, Grace Road Church Ministries, 2019)
Devi Titus, *Home Experience,*(Higherlife Development Service, 2009)
Barry Linton, *The Rise and Fall of the Roman Empire,* (Create Space Independent Publishing Platform, 2015)
Sandra Felton, *The Messie's Manual,* (Fleming H. Revell Company, 1983)

Chapter 9
Ruth Hulburt Hamilton, "Song for a Fifth Child," (Ladies Home Journal, 1958)

Chapter 10
Ruth Bell Graham, *Prodigals and Those Who Love Them,* (Baker Books, 2008)

Chapter 11
Ann Voskamp, *One Thousand Gifts,* (Zondervan, 2011)
H. A. Ray, *Curious George,* (HMH Books, 1973)

Chapter 12
Research from CircleofSecurity.com, Spokane, WA. 2018

Chapter 13
Anita Bryant, *Mine Eyes Have Seen the Glory,* (Bantam Books, January 1976)

Chapter 14
Helen Andelin, *Fascinating Womanhood*, (Pacific Press, Santa Barbara, CA)
Victor Hugo, *Les Miserables,* (1862), (film adaptation directed by Bille August 1998)

Chapter 15
Gary Chapman, *The Five Love Languages,* (Northfield Press)

Chapter 17
Gary R. Collins, Ph.D., *Christian Counseling,* (Thomas Nelson, 2006), p. 66

Chapter 18
Vance Havner, *Though I Walk through the Valley,* (Fleming H. Revell Company, 2000)
Judith Cantrell, *Notes in My Journal,* (Cantrell, 2022)
Todd Bentley, (RevivalHarvestMinistries.org)

Chapter 19
Robert Burns, "Rabbi Ben Ezra," (poem, between 1759 and 1796)
Gwen Shamblin, *The Weigh Down Diet,* (Waterbrook, 2002)
Florence Tompkins Taylor, *You Don't Have to be Old When You Grow Old*, (Bridge-Logos, 1979)

Printed in the United States
by Baker & Taylor Publisher Services